Mandate of the Anointing

Dr. Bonis E. Byrd, Jr.

TRILOGY CHRISTIAN PUBLISHERS
TUSTIN, CA

Trilogy Christian Publishers
A Wholly Owned Subsidary of Trinity Broadcasting Network
2442 Michelle Drive
Tustin, CA 92780

10 9 8 7 6 5 4 3 2 1

Library of Congress Cataloging-in-Publication Data is available.

ISBN 978-1-63769-054-3

ISBN 978-1-63769-055-0 (ebook)

Contents

CHAPTER 1

The Written Mandate

A mandate, by definition, is an authoritative order or command in writing. It usually empowers the principal with a power of attorney or trusteeship of another's property. Also, it may empower one to administer under mandate supervision and control.

It is under the auspices of the latter definition to which I wish to attribute this book. The Holy Spirit has been commissioned by the God-Head to administer and supervise through leadership, the direction, and purpose of the church in the earth.

The written mandate of the Holy Spirit is *the Holy Scripture*. Note in Romans chapter 16, verses 25 through 26, Apostle Paul in his letter to the church at Corinth states:

25 Now to him that is of power to stablish you according to my gospel, and the preaching of Jesus Christ, according to the revelation [unveiling]; of the mystery [Hidden plan], which was kept secret since the world began, 26 But now is made manifest [open to view], and by the scriptures of the prophets, according to the commandment [command or MANDATE] of the everlasting God, made known to all nations for [or to win them over to]; the obedience of faith:[1] [2]

(Emphasis added)

We see in the above passage that the written word is the revealed plan of God to *Him*, the Holy Spirit, who is able to establish you in the faith. This plan was once a secret but is now revealed to the believer as a result of the mandate of God.

In Ephesians 1:9-14, we see a further description of the mandate revealed:

9 Having made known unto us the mystery of his will, according to his good pleasure which he hath purposed in himself: 10 That in the

1 All scripture passages are presented in Authorized King James Version unless otherwise noted.

2 Comments in brackets or parentheses in AKJV passages are Author's.

dispensation of the fulness of times he might gather together in one all things in Christ, both which are in heaven, and which are on earth; even in him: 11 In whom also we have obtained an inheritance, being predestinated according to the purpose of him who worketh all things after the counsel of his own will: 12 That we should be to the praise of his glory, who first trusted in Christ. 13 In whom ye also trusted, after that ye heard the word of truth, the gospel of your salvation: in whom also after that ye believed, ye were sealed with that holy Spirit of promise, 14 Which is the earnest of our inheritance until the redemption of the purchased possession, unto the praise of his glory.

As I stated earlier in the beginning of this section, the *Mandate* is the *Holy Scriptures*, the Word of God. Therefore the Holy Spirit, The Word, and Power of God is, in fact, the *Mandate*. He (the Holy Spirit) is the revelation of God's will concerning the church.

Let's look at Ephesians 1:9:

9 Having made known unto us the mystery [Hidden plan] of His will, according to His

good pleasure which He hath purposed in Himself.

(Emphasis added)

In the Amplified Version, the Word "himself" is rendered "In Christ" [The Anointed and His Anointing, the power of God]. In other words, The Holy Spirit is the Person of God's power, the revealed Word in Him.

In Ephesians 1:10, Paul continues, "That in the dispensation of the fullness of times he might gather together in one [unity] all things in Christ..." (E)

Here we see that God's plan through the passage of time is to bring the church into unity through the power in the Anointing, both in heaven and on the earth.

In Ephesians 1:11-14, the mandate continues in that the Holy Spirit is our *guaranty* (to ensure *our inheritance* as the *purchase possession* (*the church*), we, the born-again believers who have first trusted in the presence of the Anointing in and upon us *as the Christ (Jesus)*. We also see the order of the mandate to empower the Holy Spirit with the trusteeship of the purchase possession (the church).

In the event you do not know what that inheritance is, it is further referenced in Romans 8:15-17:

15For [the Spirit which] you have now received [is]...the Spirit of adoption [the Spirit producing sonship]...16The Spirit Himself [thus] testifies together with our own spirit, [assuring us] that we are children of God. 17And if we are [His] children, then we are [His] heirs... with Christ [*sharing His inheritance with Him*], only we must share His suffering if we are to share His glory.

(AMPC) (E)

Our inheritance is the Anointing of the Anointed; we are joint-heirs with The Anointed concerning The Anointing. Do not allow your mind to be blinded to the wealth of the Anointing. In Ephesians1:3, it states:

3 Blessed be the God and Father of our lord Jesus Christ [The Anointed and His Anointing], *who hath [already] blessed us with all spiritual blessings in heavenly places [Provisions] in Christ [The Anointing of the Anointed]:*

(E)

Ephesians 3:20:

20 Now to Him [This being interpreted; The Anointing] Who, by (in consequence of) the [action of His] power that is at work within us, is able to [carry out His purpose and] do super-abundantly, far over and above all that we [dare] ask or think [infinitely beyond our

highest prayer, desires, thoughts, hopes, or dreams]

(AMPC) (E)

In these two passages above, we see that everything we need or even desire or could ever possibly conceive in our mind is available right now in the form of heavenly provisions in *the Anointing of the Anointed One*. He is able to manifest it, and if it does not exist, He is able to create it (John 15:7).

However, that which is good does not always come easy; in fact, it never comes easy, but it is obtainable. The "suffering" referenced in Romans 8, verse 17 above is referring to the believer being committed to, identifying with, and taking part in the mandate of God's plan for Christ and His family, us, the Church.

In Philippians 3:10, in the Amplified Version Classic Edition, we are given a clearer insight on this suffering:

> 10[For my determined purpose is] that I may know him [that I progressively become more deeply and intimately acquainted with Him, perceiving and recognizing and understanding the wonders of His Person more strongly and more clearly], and that I may in that same way come to know the power outflowing from His resurrection [which it exerts over believers], *and that I may so share His sufferings as to*

be continually transformed [in spirit into His like-
ness even] to His death, [in the hope]

(AMPC) (E)

We see in the above passage that Apostle Paul desired not only to know Him (the Anointing of the
Anointed) as a Person, but as the Person of Christ (the
Anointed) living in him as He (the Anointing) lived in
Christ Jesus, and to experience more and more of this
resurrected life that Christ, through His death obtained
for the Church to possess to that end. The reality of being transformed from the natural realm into the super-
natural realm, the *resurrected life* of the *resurrected Christ,*
while in this present life and willing to face every reproach, challenge (sufferings) it draws while obtaining
this goal (note Philippians 3:11).

Therefore, we see the suffering referenced in verse
10 above is the commitment to walk in a greater and
very close intimate relationship with *the Anointing of*
the Anointed, and *not* the suffering of lack, poverty, sickness, and disease as *the object.*

The Order to Empower Trusteeship

There is a further revelation of the mandate in Ephesians 3:2-21, the order (the order of *empowerment*) to reveal God's *will* to the church *through the gospel. The church*

would then, as the family of God *fully enlighten through faith and understanding*, become *trustee through Christ* (the Anointing of the Anointed). The Anointing, *the Person of God's power and love*, in and upon the church, reveals the manifold wisdom of God *through the church* to the remainder of God's creation (the angelic and heavenly host) within the universe.

A specific outline of the "Mandate" is outlined in Ephesians 4:11-16:

> 11 And he gave some, apostles; and some, prophets; and some, evangelists; and some, pastors and teachers; 12 For the *perfecting of the saints*, for the work of the ministry, for the *edifying of the body of Christ*: 13 Till we all come in *the unity of the faith*, and of the knowledge of the Son of God, *unto a perfect man*, unto the measure of *the stature of the fulness of Christ*: 14 That we henceforth be no more children, tossed to and fro, and carried about with every wind of doctrine, by the sleight of men, and cunning craftiness, whereby they lie in wait to deceive; 15 *But speaking the truth in love, may grow up into him in all things, which is the head, even Christ*: 16 From whom the whole body fitly joined together and compacted by that which every joint supplieth, according to the effectual working in the measure of every

part, maketh increase of the body unto the edifying of itself in love.

(E)

Therefore, the mandate of the Holy Spirit is summarized into four categories:

1. The *maturing* of the *Church*.
2. The *equipping* of the church for *ministry*.
3. The *unity* of the Church *in faith & understanding* of the knowledge of God with Christ being the standard.
4. The *empowerment* of the Church to mirror Christ in the earth as His body in the earth, living and revealing His Love.

It is my intention and purpose to make clear through the scriptures the aforementioned categories in a more precise, detailed description and revelation.

CHAPTER 2

The Person of the Anointing

Before we can truly explain the mandate of the Holy Spirit, we must first reveal his many faces. Let us begin with some important groundwork. The Anointing is a person, and the person is commissioned as agent. He was commissioned by the Father to rest upon and work through Jesus to reveal the truth (John 14:16-17, 26-27, 16:7, 13).

He is the third Person of the God-Head, the Holy Spirit revealed as the "might" of God's power, and God as Love revealed to man (Ephesians 3:14-19). More accurately identified, He is God's Inner-Person in the earth, through His presence in and upon you (Ephesians 3:17-19).

He is the power that empowered Jesus and enabled Him to minister without measure (Acts 10:38, John 3:34 (AMP)). That ministry and power was the work of the Holy Spirit's presence on and in Jesus. This presence and power was and is identified as *the Holy Spirit, the Anointing*.

In Ephesians 3:20, Paul lets us know that the same Anointing will enable us to do the same wonders if we will not limit him by our own abilities and sense knowledge, or "lack of the faith of Jesus Christ" (Galatians 2:20). "...Now to him that is of power to stablish you..." (Romans 16:25), that "him" in the preceding passage quoted is *the Anointing, the Spirit, and power of God*. Roman 1:16 states, "For I am not ashamed of the gospel of Christ: For it is the Power of God..." To further support my claim, we see in Ephesians 3:14 through 17(a):

> 14 For this cause I bow my knees unto the Father of our Lord Jesus Christ, 15 Of whom the whole family in heaven and earth is named, 16 That he would grant you, according to the riches of his glory, to be strengthened with might by his Spirit in the inner man; 17 That Christ [the Anointing of the Anointed] may dwell in your hearts by faith...
>
> (E)

That word "Christ" (above passage) refers to the *Anointing of the Anointed—the Spirit of Christ* as it is indicated in Romans 8:9-11.

In Ephesians 3:17, Paul was not praying that the Physical person of Jesus dwells in you but *the Spirit* that abided *on and in* Jesus, "Christ," the Anointing, the Power of God, the same power that *anointed* Jesus and *enabled Him* to fulfill God's purpose in His life.

In fact, let me go so far as to say, it was *the Anointing* that put *the Christ [the Anointing]* in and upon Jesus. See, the word "Christ" is a Greek word; it was *never translated* in the King James Bible to its English rendering. It was kept *religious*, and because of this, we accepted the word as Jesus' last name or some symbolic religious title. We have *religiously* defined "Christ" as His position and rank in relation to God when, in fact, it is *He who is The Anointed of God*. "Christ" also reveals one's *abilities and purpose*. The *Anointing* is the *unique qualifier* in and upon the believer that separates the believer above anyone else in the world.

> 5 Ye also, as lively stones, are built up a spiritual house, an holy priesthood, to offer up spiritual sacrifices, acceptable to God by Jesus Christ *[the Anointed and His Anointing]*...9 But ye are a chosen generation, a royal priesthood, an holy nation, a peculiar people; that ye should shew forth the praises of him who hath called you out of darkness into his marvellous light; 10 Which in time past were not a

people, *but are now the people of God:* which had not obtained mercy, but now have obtained mercy.

1 Peter 2:5 (E)

Anointed With What?

The word "Christ" in Hebrew means "Messiah"; in English, that means the "Anointed One," The Equipped one, the one qualified to do the job. You might ask, "Anointed with what, or equipped with what or qualified with what?" The answer is, The Power of God, The Christ; in other words, the Anointing was and is God on flesh, doing things only God can do. This power was revealed to the prophet Isaiah in Isaiah 10:27:

> 27 And it shall come to pass in that day, that his burden shall be taken away from off thy shoulder, and his yoke from off thy neck and the yoke shall be destroyed because of the anointing

Let us look into what is being stated here. First of all, this anointing will be able to move his [Satan's] burden from off your shoulders, and in addition to this, the anointing will *destroy [annihilate, extinguish all hope, make irreparable]* the yoke from off your neck. Therefore to distinguish the presence of the anointing, we should see burdens removed and yokes destroyed. This means that Jesus, as the *Anointed One*, was equipped with, or anointed with "the burden removing, yoke destroying power of God."

In Luke 4:18 (AMP) records, Jesus states His qualification: "The Spirit of the Lord [is] upon me, because he has *anointed me [the Anointed One, the Messiah, the One with burden removing, yoke destroying power]...*"

It is recorded in Acts 10:38, Apostle Peter states Jesus' qualification:

> 38 How God anointed Jesus of Nazareth *with the Holy Ghost and with power: who went about doing good, and healing all that were oppressed of the devil; for God [His Anointing] was with Him [the Anointed].*
>
> (E)

This leaves us with another eye-opening reality that if we call ourselves "Christians" (Christ-like, or Anointed like Him), then we are stating that we are "burden removing, yoke destroying, power of God believers, Anointed like Him" (Acts 11:26[c]).

Translate Then Meditate

Para-phrasing one of my spiritual mentors, It would do you well to practice stating the word "Christ" in the translated form, "The Anointing," or "The Anointed [One, optional]." In relation to "Jesus," depending on its position, the word "Christ," for example, the phrase "Jesus Christ" should be stated, "Jesus, the Anointed [One, optional] and/through His Anointing" or "Jesus, the Anointed One and His Anointing." The phrase "Christ Jesus" in most cases should be stated, "The Anointing and/or of the Anointed, Jesus" or "The Anointing and His Anointed [Jesus, optional]" or The Anointing of The Anointed [Jesus, optional]."

When the word "Christ" is found alone, through careful study, you will be able to determine how you should state or read it, For example, "The Anointing" or the Power of God, in relation to the article and/or "The Anointing of the Anointed [One, optional]." Another instance is "The Anointing through the Anointed [One]," or "The Anointing and His Anointed [One]."

However, there are some unique occasions where the word "Christ" replaces the article (i.e., 2 Timothy 2:19). In those cases, the word "Christ" translates into "The Anointed [One]." In Galatians 2:20, we see both cases can and should be used:

20 I am crucified with Christ *[The Anointed [One]]*: nevertheless I [Paul] live; yet not I (Paul), but *Christ [The Anointing/His Anointing]* liveth in me: and the life which I now live in the flesh I live by the faith of the Son of God, who loved me, and gave himself for me.

(E)

In the New Testament, you will see the word "Christ" (The Anointing) frequently inter-changed between the article and the believers. Keep in mind the passage, "And the disciples were called *Christians* first in Antioch" (Acts 11:26). Why? They were identified with Christ because they were doing the things the Anointed One did through the Anointing (Luke 4:37, 7:19-23). He healed the sick (Matthew 9:35), so did the Christian[s] (Acts 8:5-8). He opened the eyes of the blind (John 9:1-11), so did the Christian[s] (Acts 9:10-20). He healed the lame (Mark 2:3-12), so did the Christian[s] (Acts 3:1-9), and He raised the dead (Mark 5:35-43), and so did the Christian[s] (Acts 9:36-43).

And before His ascension, He (Jesus) stated:

Verily, verily, I say unto you, He that believeth *[in the anointing]* on me, the works that I do shall he *[the believer]* do also [through the anointing]; and greater works than these shall he *[the anointing]* do; because I go unto my Father *(allowing the Anointing to come and empower you; the Church)*. And whatsoever ye shall ask *[placing a demand upon the anointing]* in my name, that will I do *[through the anointing, upon and in you, the Church]*, *[so]* that the Father may be glorified in the Son [through the Church].

John 14:12-13

John the Divine stated, "because as He is, so are we in this [present] world..." (1 John 4:17).

God's Word will begin to open up to you in a totally new clarity when you begin to practice the translating of the word "Christ" in your Bible reading and study.

CHAPTER 3

The Dispensation of the Anointing

Jesus Commissioned the Holy Spirit (Anointing)

In John 14:16, Jesus says:

> And I will pray (ask) the Father, and He shall give you another Comforter (Counselor, Helper, Advocate, Intercessor, Strengthener, and Standby), that He may abide with you forever...ye know Him for *He dwelleth [dwells] with you, and shall be in you. I will not leave you comfortless [as orphans].*
>
> (E)

This Comforter is the Anointing; He is sent by Jesus to continue His work in the earth through His earthly body, the Church (Ephesians 1:18-23), which until now was done on our behalf through Jesus the Anointed.

Now in this passage (John 14:16), He prepares the disciples for the not so distant future where they and those that receive their message (the Gospel of the kingdom) would continue His work of the ministry through the Anointing abiding in and upon us.

> 7 Nevertheless I tell you the truth; It is expedient (profitable; good, advantageous) for you that I go away: for if I go not away, the Comforter *[The Anointing on Me; My Counselor, Helper, Advocate, Intercessor, Strengthener, and Standby]* will not come unto [in your behalf to abide on and have close fellowship with] you *[the same as with me]*...13 When He, the Spirit of Truth, is come, he will guide you into all [the full] truth *[for He knows (is Knower of) all things]*:...He shall not speak of Himself [His own message of His own authority] but whatsoever He shall hear *[from The Father, He will give the message that has been given to Him]* that shall He speak and He will shew *[reveal to]* you things to come *[that will happen in the future]*.
>
> John 16:7, 13-15 (E)

He further states in the following passages (I paraphrase), "whatever is His is ours..." Note verses 14 through 15:

14 He shall glorify [honor and lift me up] for He shall receive of *[draw upon that which is]* mine, and shall shew *[reveal what is mine]* unto you. 15 All things the Father hath are mine: Therefore said I *[that was my meaning when I said]*, that He shall take of *mine,* and shall shew *[reveal what is mine]* unto you *[as yours; the Church also]*.

(E)

There are two *key possessions* implied in the above text: (1) the right to be anointed like Him, and (2) what is equally His is equally ours, the believer. We have a *right*, as believers, to be "Anointed like Him" (Romans 8:17).

In Luke 24:49, Jesus commands the disciples to tarry in Jerusalem until they are *endued with power*. As born-again believers, the disciples were *legal candidates qualified to be so empowered* (John 17:19-22). This power was the anointing of God, which He preached and lived before them (Luke 4:14 through 21, Acts 10:38) and expected them to do the same (Acts 1:8). In John 15:26, Jesus says:

26 But when the Comforter is come, whom I will send unto you from the Father, *even* the Spirit of Truth, which proceedeth *[proceeds]*

from the Father, He shall testify of me [My mes-
sages and purposes for the Church].

(E)

Jesus Commissioned the Disciples

Although the disciples were the first followers of
Christ Jesus and are considered the first members of
the Church through the new covenant, we must keep in
mind that Jesus, their teacher, was *ministering under the
old covenant.*

Therefore when Jesus gave them the mission to go to
the "lost sheep of Israel" (Matthew 10th Chapter), this
was indeed *the commissioning of the disciples* to reach out
to His people also, in fact, prepare the people for His
message: "the kingdom of heaven is at hand."

The phrase "the kingdom of heaven" refers to the ad-
vent of the Power and Authority of God upon those that
would receive the Gospel of Jesus Christ or the Gospel
of the kingdom, it was also the fulfilling of the old covenant and the entrance of the new covenant, which
would ratify the old covenant through the death, burial
and resurrection of Jesus Christ (the Anointed Jesus).

Christ commissioned the disciples and anointed
them with the power and authority (Matthew 28:18-19).
Therefore, through this kingdom authority of heaven,
they "heal the sick, cleanse the lepers, raise the dead,

and cast out devils"—all of the aforementioned revealed and gave evidence of the power and authority of God.

This power and authority would rest upon and abide within every believer of the Gospel, the Church (Acts Chapter 2). The following narrative in this section reflects this truth, which is subsequent to Jesus' passion (death, burial, and resurrection of Jesus Christ).

In Mark 16:15, Jesus is recorded as saying, "Go ye into all the world, and preach the gospel..." The gospel is the good news that the kingdom of God is at hand, which is the availability of the Anointing and His Anointed "to every creature." It continues, "He that believeth" that Jesus is the Anointed "and is baptized" into that same Anointing "shall be saved." That is, healed of every sickness, delivered from every curse, to be prosperous, and established in soundness of life..."But he that believeth not shall be damned [or condemned]," due to their crime not to believe that the anointing will "remove every burden and destroy every yoke of sin."

What made this possible? "For what the law could not do, God sent forth His Son in the image of sinful flesh to condemn sin through the flesh" (Romans 8:3). The preceding scripture text alludes to its preceding verse (Romans 8:2), "the Law of the Spirit of life in Christ," the Anointing and His Anointed Jesus could make us free. The Anointing makes us free from "the law of sin and death" (Romans 8:1), which reigns as king, as a yoke of bondage in the lives of those who refuse to believe (Note Romans chapter 8 and Romans chapter 7).

In Mark 16:17, Jesus said, "And these signs shall follow [or accompany] them that believe" in the burden removing yoke destroying power of God; the Anointing, "...In my name" through which they are given *Power of Attorney*, "...shall they cast out devils, they shall speak with new tongues..." Even if "they shall take up serpents [unaware]..." and if "they drink any deadly thing [unaware],...it shall not hurt them; they shall lay hands... [anointed to heal]...on the sick, and they...[who through faith, believe in that healing anointing]...shall recover."

This message (Gospel of the kingdom) was to be taught by the disciples and all those that believed through their message. As they preached this message, the Lord, through His Anointing, would confirm the anointed word, which they preached with *signs and wonders following*.

Note Acts 5:8, where Philip went down to Samaria and preached Christ [the Anointed and His Anointing] to them, and the Anointing would confirm the anointed Word which he preached with various types of healing and deliverance to those oppressed of devils, and as a result, there was "great joy" in that city.

I want to make clear that the phrase "preached Christ" implied that he preached *the message Jesus preached, the gospel of the kingdom*. Although it is not taught and boldly proclaimed enough, that in Matthew 28:19, where Jesus instructs the disciples to "teach all nations, baptizing them in the name of the Father, and of the Son, and of the Holy Ghost..." the message to be taught was "The Gospel of the Kingdom" (Matthew 13:10-17, Acts 8:5-8, Romans 14:17), and "the Anointed and His Anointing, the burden removing, yoke destroying power" on Jesus, and then *baptize and anoint the believer in that Anointing*.

The disciples were to minister this message (Gospel of the Kingdom) and baptize by the authority of and in the name of the Father, *the source of the Anointing*, and in the name of the Son, *who was the First Begotten of the Anointing*, and in the name of the Holy Ghost (Spirit) *who is here to confirm*.

Note Ephesians 3:20-21 (AMP):

> 20[a]...by [in consequence of] the [action of His] power that is at work within us...

Note "the power...within us" to do only those things that only God on flesh can do, and He alone.

> 20[b]...is able to [carry out His purpose]...

Note, "His purpose" is the purpose of the Anointing upon the Anointed Jesus, *or an anointed one like Him*, a believer of the Anointed Word

20[c]...do superabundantly, far over and above all that we [dare] ask or think [infinitely beyond our highest prayers, desires, thoughts, hopes, or dreams]—

21[a] To Him be glory in the church...

Note, "The Church," *the governing body* of believers baptized into the Anointing's *"Mandate,"*

21[b]...and in Christ Jesus...

Note, "In Christ Jesus," the Anointing of the Anointed Jesus,

21[c]...throughout all generations...

Note, "All generations," of every ethnicity (nations),

21[d]...forever and ever. Amen (so be it).

All the disciples' message was the same; they preached "Christ" the Anointed and His Anointing. Peter at the gate of the temple called "Beautiful," through the power of the Anointing, raised the man lame from his birth. The people marveled at what had taken place in the life of him that was lame. But Peter and John were quick to make clear to the people that it was "the power of the Anointing" (Acts 3:1 through 4:12).

Saul, after his Damascus road experience (Acts 9:1-9), was visited by Ananias, a disciple of Christ, who laid hands upon him that he might receive his sight (Acts 9:10-18). Afterward, he visited with the disciples a small period of time while they made plain the scriptures unto him in regards to Jesus and His Anointing (Acts 9:19). In verse 20 of the ninth chapter of Acts, we see him immediately preaching "Christ" the Anointed and His Anointing to all who would hear him in the synagogues.

Peter was sent to Cornelius, a Roman Centurion who believed in God and supported the preaching of the Gospel through the giving of his finances (Acts 10:1-2). Peter, upon his arrival at Cornelius' home, began to preach the Word (The Anointing and His Anointed (Acts 10:24-29, 34-38)). While he preached the Anointing, the Holy Ghost fell upon all of them, which heard the Anointed Word (Acts 10:44-48).

As a result of this obedience to the commission of Jesus Christ, the Anointed and His Anointing, the church was scattered through persecution. However, everywhere the church was scattered, the Anointing was being preached.

There was one such church in Antioch composed of and led by Simeon, nicknamed "Niger the Black" (a Latin word written in the gospel using Greek letters) (Acts

13:1-3); he was joined by Apostle Paul and Barnabas, who taught in the church, along with other prophets and teachers for a space of one year. As a result of this teaching (Acts 11:22-26, 13:1-3), the church went about the ministry, doing many things that Jesus performed in His earthly ministry. Because of their success in the spreading of the Word (the acts and teachings of the Anointed and His Anointing), as the hearers received the word in their hearts, they received the Anointing with signs manifesting in their life accordingly. Their lifestyle and conviction in the Word resulted in them being called "Christians" (Anointed like Him [Jesus]) first at this church in Antioch.

Jesus Commissioned the Church

In Matthew 28:18-20, we see the great commission of the Church, the body of Christ in the earth. This is *the empowerment of the church*, although many of us have yet to walk in or activate it in our lives.

18 And Jesus came and spake unto them, saying, All power is given unto me in heaven and in earth. 19 Go ye therefore, and teach all nations, baptizing them in the name of the Father, and of the Son, and of the Holy Ghost: 20 Teaching them to observe all things what-

soever I have commanded you: and, lo, I am with you always, even unto the end of the world. Amen.

I always find it important to indicate two unique points in the above passages (Matthew 28:18-20). Firstly, in verse 18, Jesus states: "All power has been given unto me in heaven and in earth..." This clearly indicates Jesus' victory over Satan, and his satanic host was ended, their authority over man. Every man, based on this victory obtained through Jesus' death, burial, and resurrection, is *potentially saved*. This salvation is based upon mankind taking advantage of the salvation offered them. Not one demon, devil, or Satan himself can prevent any man from coming to Christ because Christ has redeemed man from Satan's authority (Galatians 3:13-14, Romans 8:1-4) upon hearing and receiving the Gospel of Jesus Christ (Romans 10:8-11).

From this point on, man can choose salvation or damnation. Now and henceforth, man can choose salvation by acting upon the Word (Romans 10:9-10) or choose damnation by lack of action, remaining in sin and unbelief; it is man's choice.

Secondly, in the above passage (Matthew 28:18-20), in verse 19 Jesus states, "...go ye therefore..." The point projected here is *the revelation* that Christ did not reflect the disciples as "dis-joint" from Himself but literally

MANDATE OF THE ANOINTING

and spiritually "joined" a part of Him, *His body in the earth* (the Church). Therefore it was not necessary, or it would be redundant to say "...take my authority..." to one's own *self* or *body*, or take what you *already possess or been given.*

What Christ Jesus possesses, the Church possesses:

> 13 Howbeit when he, the Spirit of truth, is come, he will guide you into all truth: for he shall not speak of himself; but whatsoever he shall hear, that shall he speak: and he will shew you things to come. 14 He shall glorify me: for he shall receive of mine, and shall shew it unto you. 15 All things that the Father hath are mine: therefore said I, that he shall take of mine, and shall shew it unto you.
>
> John 16:13-15

In addition, we see the Church is the body of Christ in the earth:

> 17 That the God of our Lord Jesus Christ, the Father of glory, may give unto you *the spirit of wisdom and revelation in the knowledge of him:* 18 *The eyes of your understanding being enlight-ened;* that ye may know what is *the hope of his calling,* and what the riches of *the glory of his inheritance in the saints,* 19 And what is the ex-

ceeding greatness of his power to us-ward [toward us] who believe, according to the working of his mighty power, 20 Which he wrought in Christ [The Anointed], when he raised him from the dead, and set him at his own right hand in the heavenly places, 21 Far above all principality, and power, and might, and dominion, and every name that is named, not only in this world, but also *in that which is to come:* 22 And hath put all things under his feet, and *gave him to be the head over all things to [or concerning] the church,* 23 *Which is his body [in the earth], the fulness of him that filleth all in all [we are complete in Him, and He is complete in us in the earth].*

Ephesians 1:17-23 (E)

As the body of Christ, the Church is anointed with His power, authority, and anointing. *Henceforth, the Church is equipped to be commissioned* to carry out *God's Mandate* (Note Ephesians 3:9-10 (AMP). Short of His body, the Church, the Anointing can do nothing in the earth. Therefore, the new birth qualifies us, the believers, to grow in the "wisdom and revelation in the knowledge of him" (Ephesians 1:17); we become the enlightened Church to enlighten God's creation by His Anointing in and upon us, the body of Christ in the earth (Ephesians 1:18, 20-23, 3:10-12 (see AMP)).

CHAPTER 4

Christ His Body in the Earth

The Church the Body of Christ

According to Ephesians, the Church is the body of Christ in the earth, and as the body of Christ, the Church is anointed with His power, authority, and anointing. *Henceforth, the Church is equipped to be commissioned* to carry out *God's Mandate*; note Ephesians 3:9-10 (AMP). *Short of His body, the Church, the Anointing can do nothing in the earth.* Therefore, the new birth qualifies us, the believer to grow in the "wisdom and revelation in the knowledge of him" (Ephesians 1:17); we become an enlightened Church to enlighten God's creation through His Anointing in and upon us, *the body of Christ in the earth* (Ephesians 1:18, 20-23, 3:10-12 (see AMP)).

The Anointing Empowers the Church

In Philippians 2:13, Paul states,

13 For it is God which worketh in you both to will and to do of his good pleasure.

Here, Paul reveals to us that the *purpose of the Anointing* is to empower us, the Church. And through his power, the Anointing, and the love of God, we are filled with the enthusiasm to build our relationship to *carry out his mandate*. In fact, we are only limited by our lack of establishing *a personal relationship with the Spirit of God* to press in and acquaint ourselves with Him, the Anointing of the Anointed (Philippians 3:10).

Through Paul's determined purpose to acquaint himself with the Anointing was how he became acquainted with *the Anointing's mandate*. This mandate became Paul's calling to reveal the *hidden plan* of God to the Church (Ephesians 3:4-11[AMP]).

Paul possessed an unquenchable desire to know the anointing, and it was revealed in Philippians 3:10:

10 *[For my determined purpose is]* that I may know Him *[that I may progressively become more deeply and intimately acquainted with Him, perceiving and recognizing and understanding the*

wonders of His Person more strongly and more clearly], and that I may *in that same way come to know the power outflowing from His resurrection [which it exerts over believers], and that I may so share His sufferings as to be continually transformed [in spirit into His likeness even]* to His death, [in the hope]

(AMP) (E)

Paul knew that it was the anointing that empowered Jesus, and if he knew the anointing with the *same close fellowship*, there would be absolutely nothing that he could not do.

13[a] I have strength for all things *in Christ Who empowers me* [I am ready for anything and equal to anything *through Him Who infuses inner strength into me...*]

Philippians 4:13[a] (AMP) (E)

Remember, the anointing literally means *God on Flesh doing things only God can do.* The 13th verse continues:

13[b]...I am self-sufficient in Christ's sufficiency

Philippians 4:13[b] (AMP)

The more we know the Anointing through close fellowship, the less effort is required in our own strength to accomplish the will of God. Jesus said in John 15:5:

> 5 I am the vine, ye are the branches: He that abideth in me *[live in me and my Anointing]*, and I *[I and the Anointing as one and the same]* in him, the same bringeth forth much fruit [through a submitted life]: *for without me ye can do nothing.*
>
> (E)

To "abide" in the above scripture passage infers, to live as a way of life, to become a state common to you, a life of fellowship, an active relationship as inferred in John 15:7:

> 7 If you abide in [live an active life of fellowship with] me [and the anointing on me] and my words [of the Anointed gospel] abide in [live and has its place in] you, ye shall ask *[demanding and declaring]* what you will *[through that same Anointing]* and it *[the Anointed words of your demand, declaring]* shall be done *[or created, if necessary through the anointing]* unto you *[in your behalf]*.
>
> (E)

Jesus' close fellowship with the Anointing enabled Him to *minister without measure* (Matthew 9:27-30, Mark 10:46-52) on behalf of those that believed in Him *as the Anointed of the Anointing (literally the Messiah)*. Paul's close fellowship with the anointing created a reputation that put fear in the spirits of darkness. Note Acts 19:13-16:

> 13 Then certain of the vagabond [traveling] Jews, *exorcists*, took upon them to call over [speak over] them which had evil spirits [in] the name of the LORD Jesus, saying, We adjure [command and charge] you by Jesus whom Paul preacheth. 14 And there were seven sons of one Sceva, a Jew, and chief of the priests, which did so. 15 *And the evil spirit answered* and said, *Jesus I know, and Paul I know; but who are ye?* 16 And the man in whom *the evil spirit* was *leaped on them, and overcame them, and prevailed against them, so that they fled out of that house naked and wounded.*
>
> (E)

Philip went down to Samaria and preached Christ (The Anointed and His Anointing) to them. And he, through his close fellowship with the anointing, delivered many in the city, causing the city to express great joy. I say, no one can do this except "God be with him."

Isn't that what Nicodemus said to Jesus on a certain occasion (John 3:2)?

Therefore, we see that the Holy Spirit (The Anointing) empowered believers to perform the same as Jesus as they sought close fellowship with Him. And no doubt this reality of thought was included and stressed in many of Paul's teaching at Antioch (Acts 11:22-26). These believers at Antioch were called or identified as *Christians* or "anointed ones, like Him" (Jesus the Anointed and His Anointing).

I believe they obtained this name "Christian" as a direct result of not only what they preached but as a result of how they lived. These believers lived a life of meditating the scriptures and a life of prayer and fellowship of the Holy Spirit. These believers got to know the power of the Anointing in their life, as they were taught and encouraged by Paul, Barnabas, and Niger, who were the teachers of the Antioch believers (Acts 13:1-3). According to Acts chapter 11, verses 22 through 26, they were the first of the church to be identified with the Anointing of the Anointed Jesus.

Note John 3:34:

> 34 For he whom God hath sent speaketh the words of God: for God giveth not the Spirit by measure *unto him*. 35 The Father loveth the Son, and hath given all things into his hand.

The important note to be made concerning this passage is that often this passage has been taught by reference to Jesus the Messiah *only*, but through careful study, it is clear the phrase *"unto him"* is in Italics, which means concerning the Authorized King James Version of the Bible (the text referenced above), the "Italics" are added by the translator. The Italics are not a part of the original scripture or text.

Thus we can conclude, based on *original intent*, the anointing is distributed without measure to the recipient; in this case, *Christ and those who believe in him as the Messiah [Anointed].* This conviction can be further confirmed in that it is in the same area where Jesus introduces Himself to Nicodemus as the Messiah, and the things that he taught concerning the kingdom require being born of the Spirit of God. This new birth qualifies the believer to salvation and the Anointing of God abiding in and upon him.

I always like to use the following analogy: when you get into your car or any vehicle of conveyance, how much of you get into the conveyance? The answer is, no doubt, all of you or your entire body. Well, that is what happens when you are born of the Spirit of God, when He, the Holy Spirit, enters or comes into your life, all of the Holy Spirit inhabits your being.

Acquainting the Church with the Mandate

The mandate of the Holy Spirit was never intended to be carried out without the involvement of the church (the family of God in the earth). The mandate of the Holy Spirit included the church as the vehicle in which the whole entire universe would be enlightened. Ephesians 3:10 through 12:

> 10 To the intent [purpose] that now unto the principalities and powers in heavenly places might be known by [or rather, through] the church the manifold [many faceted sides of the] wisdom of God, 11 According to the eternal purpose which he purposed in Christ [the Anointing and His Anointed] Jesus our Lord: 12 In whom we have boldness [confidence] and access with confidence by the faith of him.
>
> (E)

So we see that without the church walking in the state and intent of original creation, the above passage could not be.

According to the above passage, *the born-again man* as the Church, and through the purposed "mandate" of the Christ [Anointed and His Anointing], man will be re-instated to his legal position, *authority over God's cre-*

ation. Therefore, the Church will be able to reveal God's glory to the entire universe, *God's creation.*

The *born-again* man will be in *authority over God's creation.* This new man, as the Church, will be in dominion over every living thing *except the God-Head* and *one another.* And, if I might add, *the dominion of the church is the only legal dominion that exists in the earth.* Remember, Jesus took back that which was stolen, He entered Satan's domain *(the current world's system)* and made a show of him openly *in his own domain*; note Colossians 2:10-15:

> 10 And ye are complete in him, which is the head of all principality and power: 11 in whom also ye are circumcised with the circumcision made without hands *[a better covenant of better promises]*, in putting off the body of the sins of the flesh by the circumcision of Christ: 12 buried with him in baptism, wherein also ye are risen with him *[identify as a new creature through his resurrected life]* through the faith of the operation of God, who hath raised him from the dead *[therefore you are alive to the new life in him].* 13 And you, being dead in your sins and the uncircumcision of your flesh, hath he quickened together with him, having forgiven you all trespasses; 14 Blotting out the handwriting of ordinances that was

against us, which was contrary to us, and
took it out of the way, nailing it to his cross; 15
And having spoiled principalities and powers,
he made a shew of them openly, triumphing
over them in It [*that is, he displayed them before
all creation and that which is their domain, this
current world's system, through the first Adam,
and now overthrown through the obedience of the
last Adam, and defeated them, in your behalf*].

(E)

The wisdom of God in the Church, its spiritual
knowledge and involvement was a necessary require-
ment, or God's mandate could not be legal. The church
is the body of Christ (the Anointing) in the realm of the
natural (Ephesians 1:17-23). And, the Church is adopted
by the Holy Spirit, "The Spirit of Adoption" (Romans
8:15), which made us heirs of God, the Creator of the
Universe and joint-heirs with Jesus Christ [*The Anointed, His Son and we, as sons and joint-heirs to His Anointing*].
The Anointing's only way to carry out *His Mandate* was
being inside of *a willing, obedient, and spiritually enlightened Church.*

In the eyes of God, Jesus' death, burial, and resurrection redeemed man for the purpose of establishing his
Church; the Church is composed of those that believed
and accepted the death, burial, and resurrection of Je-

sus Christ as their redemption from Satan and sin. As the Church, we are *reinstated* to our *original intent*. The Church is the body of Christ in the earth in our rightful position, in right-standing with God through Jesus Christ (The Anointed and His Anointing).

> 21 For our sake He made Christ [virtually] to be sin who knew no sin, so that in *and* through Him we might become [endued with, viewed as being in, and examples of] the righteousness of God [what we ought to be, approved and acceptable and in right relationship with Him, by His goodness]
> 2 Corinthians 5:21 (AMP) (E)

All throughout the Old Testament, we see the heartfelt desire of God to *reinstate man to this position of right relationship with Himself:* "And I shall be your God, and you shall be my people" (Psalm 103:22). God's heartfelt desire is realized through His Son's victory over Satan, the god of this present world, in its fallen state (2 Corinthians 4:3-4):

> 3 But if our gospel be hid, it is hid to them that are lost: 4 In whom the god of this world hath blinded the minds of them which believe not, lest the light of the glorious gospel of Christ,

who is the image of God, should shine unto them.

Now the church, God's new nation, and family are workers together with Him the Anointing, reconciling the World (its inhabitants) back to God as His Ambassadors. The Old Covenant is fulfilled, and the New Covenant is the active involvement of the Holy Spirit at work in and through the church today. *Every man is potentially saved;* yes, redemption is available to every man. Through this mighty act of God through Jesus Christ, all those willing to receive this gift and become the purchase possession (the Church), we will actively participate with the Holy Spirit in reconciling the world back to God. And upon the reinstatement of the believer into the Church, they will become fellow dominators of God's creation as God had intended before the foundation of the world.

The first step of walking in dominion requires the church to relate to the *Holy Spirit as a person, God's Inner-Man.* Jesus foretold the disciples that He would send them another *Comforter.* Now they did not fully understand Jesus' words (John chapters 14 through 16), and as a result, during the crucifixion of Christ, it is recorded that the church was in *a state of fear and unbelief.* The disciples, as recorded in Mark chapter 16, verses 1 through 14, on several different occasions express their fear and unbelief of His (Jesus') resurrection; even when seen by a couple of the disciples themselves, the rest of them still refused to believe.

However, in Mark 16:15-16, we see an entirely different group of men being commission by the Lord: "Go ye into all the world, and preach the gospel to every creature...He that believeth...shall be saved..." Something took place between passages 14 and 15 of Mark chapter 16 to move these men from *fear and unbelief to faith and boldness.*

In Luke 24th chapter verses 36 through 49, we see the same account referenced by Mark. However, in this account, we see where He declared *His Peace be theirs.* The *Spirit of Peace* is another name for the *Anointing* (John 14:26 through 27). The disciples' reception of the *Spirit of Peace* reconciles them to God, and God becomes a Father to them (2 Corinthians 6:16-18). Jesus endued them with the *Spirit of Peace,* and they became *spirit-filled believers in Him and His Anointing.*

Afterwards, Jesus, upon them receiving the Spirit, began to open their understanding to the scriptures, how they spoke of Him and how He had to fulfill the scriptures (Luke 24:6-7, 25-27, 44-48). His teaching makes their understanding clearer to the scriptures. Later, He commissions them by instructing them to give witness to these events. But they were required to tarry or wait in Jerusalem until they are baptized in the

Holy Ghost [Spirit] and with *the power* to witness under *the same anointing* as He ministered while among them (Luke 24:49).

Men born of the Spirit become *eligible to receive spiritual knowledge and spiritual power.* Men become eligible to mature in the things of God. As offspring's of God, *they take on his attributes and walk in the true identity of who they are*—anointed spirit-filled, spirit-led "Sons of God."

In John 21:19, we note John's account of the same period. Upon Jesus' appearance before them, he revealed who He was (God's Anointed Son) and put them at peace in the revelation of God's plan *(the mandate concerning the Church)* through His death, burial and resurrection as God's Anointed, the *first-born of the Church* (Ephesians 1:10, 9-14). Upon this revelation, *the disciples received the Holy Spirit* themselves and became the *first members of the Church of God in Christ* and shared this universal message (1 Corinthians 1:2).

Now we come to the Book of Acts. The Holy Spirit comes on the scene as promised by the Lord (Acts 1:4,8), the disciples are to be *endued with power from on high,* the God-kind of ability to be witnesses on His behalf. They are introduced to the greatest power on the face of the earth (Acts 2:1-4). For the first time, the Holy Spirit, God's Anointing, is no longer just visiting upon man for a brief period, but now *to abide upon and dwell within man* as His temple. He (as The Anointing) now abides and exists in the born again man as *the Inner-Man of God Himself*.

He (the Anointing) is now *the character of God Himself and the very personality of Jesus Christ (the Anointed-One)* in the believer. The disciples can be just like their *covenant big brother*, "a friend [covenant-friend] that sticketh closer than a brother [of natural birth and from the same womb]..." They are legal candidates by right of the new birth of the Spirit.

This brings about the *second step* of the Holy Spirit; they shall know *the fellowship of Holy Spirit*; they shall *know Him even as He was known of Jesus in His earthly ministry*. The Holy Spirit will be known of the believers as *the One who put the Anointing in and upon Jesus in His earthly ministry*. The believers will *no longer be limited* by their fallen nature, now dead (or rather unemployed). They can only be *limited by their lack of fellowship of the Anointing* (John 14:16-21).

The Apostle Paul was commissioned to make the *Mandate of the Anointing* known to the church (Ephesians 1:1-14), to reveal the heartfelt desire of the Holy Spirit, to be known of the church, to be known as *the One who put the Christ in the Church*. Through Him (the Anointing of the Anointed), the Church would be known as the *Anointed-Ones (Christ-ians, Anointed ones like Him)*; Anointed of God: "Christ in you, the hope of Glory..." (Colossians 1:27[b])

45

The Church would now be able to reveal God's will to the world and all principalities and existing authorities the manifold wisdom of God. Note Ephesians 3:9-12:

> 9...and to make plain [to everyone] the plan of the mystery [regarding the uniting of believing Jews and Gentiles into one body] which [until now] was kept hidden through the ages in [the mind of] God who created all things. 10 So now through the church the multifaceted wisdom of God [in all its countless aspects] might now be made known [revealing the mystery] to the [angelic] rulers and authorities in the heavenly *places*. 11 *This is* in accordance with [the terms of] the eternal purpose which He carried out in Christ Jesus our Lord, 12 in whom we have boldness and confident access through faith in Him [that is, our faith gives us sufficient courage to freely and openly approach God through Christ].
>
> (AMP)

I would like to point out that this "mystery" or "hidden plan" referenced in the passage above is a mystery or plan *kept hidden for you, not from you.*

CHAPTER 5

The Mandate of Revelation

The Spirit of Truth Revealed

In John the 16th chapter, verse 13, it states:

> 13...But when the Friend comes, the Spirit of the Truth, he will take you by the hand and guide you into all the truth there is. He won't draw attention to himself, but will *make sense out of what is about to happen* and, indeed, out of all that I have done and said...
>
> (MSG Translation) (E)

There are some misunderstandings concerning the word "revelation," and before we proceed, it bears clarity. First of all, let's strip our minds of the *religious* perception of revelation. It has nothing to do with the future. To tell the future is to *foretell* or to speak of something that will come to pass *without any bases of support or foundation.*

In the above verse, the "Friend," the "Comforter" (AKJV), will guide us into all the truth. Truth is not related to the future. *Truth is* regardless to *past, present, or future,* and it is something that *already exists* and is *totally independent* of you or me being aware of it. Truth will not, nor can ever change. Truth is not "Facts," as "facts" often change through an increase in *knowledge and/or experiences in life and/or the given discipline or science.*

However, truth is based upon *indisputable reality,* much like mathematical laws or principles. And, based upon one's knowledge of these truths, *the outcome is predictable* or can be *determined as truth or reality.*

One must take three things into consideration when God speaks: (1) what God speaks is *truth or reality brought into existence.* In fact, what He speaks from the super-natural, is translated from the spirit or out of the Spirit of God into the natural realm where we exist; *this is truth declared.* (2) *When God declares a thing (truth),* whether we are aware of it or not, it does not discount or render it null or non-existent. However, when you come to the knowledge of it (the truth), you simply have *the truth revealed.* (3) God resides in the realm of the supernatural, which is outside of the realm of the natural where time exists, and in the supernatural where God resides, we must take into account that *the past, present, and future* exist *simultaneously* before Him.

Therefore, He (God) declares *the end* from *the beginning* (Isaiah 42:9-10):

> 9 Remember the former things of old: for I *am* God, and *there is* none else;
>
> I *am* God, and *there is* none like me,
>
> 10 *declaring the end from the beginning,*
>
> and from ancient times *the things* that are not *yet* done,
>
> saying, My counsel shall stand, and I will do all my pleasure [that I purpose].
>
> (E)

In summation, based on the above, we conclude that *God exists outside of time (the supernatural).* God created time for you and me. *Man lives, or resides, within the realm of time (the Natural or sensual realm).* I always like to state, "Since God knows all things (omniscient), he created time to give us time to catch up subsequent to the fall" (of the first Adam).

If we knew *truth or reality* through any other means, then we would not be required to "walk by faith," that is, to live by faith. Also, another aspect of *revelation* concerning *the purpose of the Bible is the Revelation of God Himself and His will for man.*

Therefore, revelation is *the disclosure of something that existed* independent of our knowledge of it. However, this truth existed and was not yet realized prior to its disclosure.

Theologically, "Revelation" is the disclosure of divine truth, or as I like to state it, "Truth revealed."

> 25 Now to him that is of power to stablish you according to my gospel, and the preaching of Jesus Christ, according to the revelation *[reveal truth]* of the mystery *[hidden plan]*, which was kept secret since the world began, 26 But now is made manifest *[brought into view]*, and by the scriptures of the prophets, according to the commandment *[laws, or will]* of the everlasting God, made known to all nations *[or ethnics]* for *[into]* the obedience of faith...
>
> Romans 16:25-26 (E)

So based on this knowledge, we can *immediately determine* that the *Holy Spirit's mandate is to reveal truth to the church.* This "Truth" that was hidden since time began but now, in the God-appointed time, He (the Holy Spirit) will reveal His purpose in, for, and through the church.

Understand this: the church is not presented in the Bible as an un-informed body (Ephesians 3:9-11), but because of the new birth, it is a new creation born of the Spirit of God for the very purpose of carrying out the long-awaited hope "Christ [the Anointing] in you the hope of glory" to fulfill a purpose:

> ...That energy is God's energy [the Anointing], an energy deep within you, God himself willing and working at what will give him the most pleasure. Do everything readily and cheerfully no bickering, no second-guessing allowed! Go out into the world uncorrupted a breath of fresh air in this squalid and polluted society. Provide people with a glimpse of good living and of the living God. Carry the light-giving Message into the night...
>
> Philippians 2:12-16[3] (MSG Translation)

The Mandate of the Anointing is *Revelation of the Holy Spirit* equipping the church through *the Anointing* to fulfill purpose in the earth as the family of God. This would require the church as the body of Christ (God's Holy family), reborn of the Spirit of God and *anointed by Him* to walk in their *true original intent and dominion*, reconciling the world back to God in total agreement with the Holy Spirit (Matthew 16:17-19, 2 Corinthians 5:14-21, Ephesians 1:3-23). To the intent, we, the church,

---

3 MSG Translation, Eugene Peterson's The Message

will usher in again the Christ (the Anointed One) for the catching up of the church, the family of God the Eternal.

The Church realizes that they are the habitation of the Holy Spirit as anointed ones like the Anointed One, Jesus. We, the believers, become the Holy Spirit's doors of access into the earth *legally*. Through His presence and power, He will, through them (the Church), preach Christ (the Anointing and His Anointed) to mankind everywhere, and go about doing good and healing all that are oppressed of the devil (Acts 10:38). In John 14:12, the Anointed One himself said, "Not only these works will you do, but greater works."

In Acts 10:38, Peter proclaimed:

> 38...How God anointed Jesus of Nazareth with the Holy Ghost and with power; who went about doing good and healing all that were oppressed of the devil for God was with Him.

How was God with Him? He was with Him through the presence of the Anointing, in and upon Him.

Therefore I declare on behalf of the Church that possess this same conviction and Anointing, "like Father, like son."

The Mandate of the Anointing is to *illuminate the Church to God's divine revelation and become the agency of God to enlighten the universe* (Ephesians 3:1-12 (AMP). This is that "better thing" referred to by the Hebrew writer in Hebrews 11:39-40, or "better plan," as stated in E. G. Peterson's *The Message:*

> Not one of these People (under the old covenant), even though their lives of faith were exemplary, got their hands on what was promised. God had a *better plan for us* (under the new covenant): that their faith and our faith would come together to make *one completed whole*, their lives of faith not complete apart from ours.
>
> (E)

His Method of Teaching

The Holy Spirit, although the greatest Teacher, requires the cooperation of the student or disciple, the church body.

In 1 John 2:20, John, the divine states:

> 2 But you have been anointed by [*you hold a sacred appointment* from, *you have been given an*

unction from] the Holy One, and you all know
[*the Truth*] or you know all things
(AMPC)

As I have heard one preacher state, "You have an unction to function," and that is exactly what it is; you have unction from the anointing of God. The anointing is your *unction to function* in the world as a child of God. Paul stated in Romans 8:8-15 (AMPC):

> 8...So then those who are living the life of the flesh [catering to the appetites and impulses of their carnal nature] cannot please or satisfy God, or be acceptable to Him. 9 But you are not living the life of the flesh, you are living *the life of the Spirit,* if the [Holy] Spirit of God [really] *dwells within you [directs and controls you].* But if anyone does not possess the [Holy] Spirit of Christ, he is none of His [he does not belong to Christ, is not truly a child of God]...12 So then, brethren, we are debtors, but not to the flesh *[we are not obligated to our carnal nature] to live [a life ruled by the standards set up by the dictates] of the flesh [we are not obligated to our carnal nature]...*13...But if through the power of the [Holy] Spirit you are [habitually] putting to death (making extinct, dead-

ening) the [evil] deeds prompted by the body, you shall [really and genuinely] live forever. 14 For all who are led by the Spirit of God are the sons of God. 15 For [the Spirit which] you have now received [is] not a spirit of slavery to put you once more in bondage to fear, but you have received the Spirit of adoption [the Spirit producing sonship] in [the bliss of] which we cry, Abba [Father]! Father!

(E)

As a child of God, you are equipped with *the Spirit of life* to live *the God kind of life*. You have no further obligation to the spirit of darkness, and neither does he. The spirit of darkness possesses no further influence over you. You have been empowered to live the spirit of life [a holy unction] through the Holy Spirit.

This new spirit life is developed through being, first, *born of the Holy Spirit*; secondly, developing an *active fellowship of the Holy Spirit*, learning His voice and personality. In fact, we are to fully submit to the Holy Spirit to live in and through us. This requires the cooperation (obedience) of each individual as Christians (Anointed ones, like Him) in order for this to be possible. The more you develop this born-again spirit life, the more you *put to death [render unemployed]* the spirit of darkness, thus becoming *mature men and women of God [sons of God]*.

Jesus' lifestyle is *the Mandate of the Holy Spirit* for every believer. Jesus implied strongly in his earthly ministry that He was here to do the will of the Father: (1) He only performed the things permitted and allowed by the Father (John 5:19-23, 30), and (2) He only spoke the Words He heard His Father speak (John 8:26-28).

Jesus' lifestyle in the earth was *being the Word, speaking the Word, Anointed by the Holy Ghost [Spirit]. This conviction* is what kept Him free to overcome every obstacle and perform every task required of Him by the Father. Likewise, this is the *"Mandate of the believer," to become the Word, speaking the Word, and Anointed by the Holy Ghost [Spirit].* The aforementioned is the lifestyle required of every believer, to know the Truth as the "unction" within to "function" as one that "overcomes" the works of darkness and "fulfill" the will of God, free indeed as Jesus declared in John 8:31-32, 34[b]-36:

> 31 Then said Jesus to those Jews which believed on him, If ye continue in my word, then are ye my disciples *indeed*; 32 And ye shall *know* the truth, and the truth shall *make you free*...34[b]...Verily, verily, I say unto you, Whosoever committeth sin is the servant of sin. 35 And *the servant abideth not* in the house for ever: but *the Son* abideth ever *[forever or*

eternally]. 36 If the *Son* therefore *shall make you free, ye shall be free indeed.*

(E)

You must continue in Him, *acknowledge His presence in you*; it is not an option. As a mentor of mine stated, "practicing the presence of God" in you. This is *the lifestyle* of the believer, *knowing His heart, hearing and obeying His voice.* The aforementioned lifestyle requires knowing the Word of God; the Spirit speaks the Word of God only (John 16:13-15). In knowing the Anointing, we know our purpose and ourselves. As one preacher stated, "If you want to know something about a car, don't ask the car, ask the manufacturer of the car."

I declare to you, if you want to know you, don't ask yourself, ask your *Maker*, and inquire within His *Operator's Manual, The Word, The Holy Bible. He* (the Anointed and His Anointing) is the Life and the Life-Giver: "I come that you may have life and that more abundantly" (John 10:10), or in other words, I come that you may experience true *spiritual* life and its abundant lifestyle, which makes and reveals true life, that is in truth. He (Jesus) is the Author of life itself (the Anointed and His Anointing).

He Will Glorify God

In John chapter 16:14, Jesus states,

> 14 He [the Anointing, the Holy Spirit in you],
> will glorify me [reflect, represent all that I
> AM, The Author of all life].
>
> (E)

This life (Holy Spirit) living through the believer
gives glory to the living God. As believers totally submitted to the Anointing, we will accomplish every task
effortlessly. Because in the Spirit, we do everything as
the Father would have it, and as we cooperate with the
Spirit, we have the backing of the whole *God-Head* op-
erating with us, and absolutely nothing can oppose us
successfully. Note 2 Corinthians 4:6-7:

> 6 For God who commanded the light to shine
> out of darkness hath shined in our hearts,
> to give the light [the illumination] of the
> knowledge of the glory of God in the face of
> Jesus Christ *[as the literal physical image and
> prototype]*. But we have this treasure [the di-
> vine Light of the Gospel; the power of the
> Anointed; His Anointing] in earthen vessels,

[so] that the excellency of the power may be
of God, and not of us.

(E)

The Anointing, the light and glory of God, that part
which makes God, God, now incarnate or better yet re-
incarnated "in earthen vessels [the Church, the body of
Christ]." God now abides in you (the body of Christ),
His spiritual wisdom and knowledge now living in you.
Now, reborn of the Spirit, you are now in your original
state and original intent (sinless and righteous before
God). God, with your cooperation, now lives through
you, that God may have earthly habitation and access in
the earth "that the Excellency" that part which is God in
you, and is understood to be identified as "the power"
of God abiding in you, God living in, upon, and through
you, and the power revealed or *shown as of God, and not
of us.*

In John 16:15, we see that He (the Anointing in you)
will reveal all that the Father possesses, which is in fact
revealing what the Son possesses, as well as the purpose and *mandate of the Holy Spirit (The Anointing in you).*

That is to say, to reveal God's purpose is to reveal
God's purpose for you and all mankind, and in that
purpose, you will have revealed *your part and provisions*
in the big picture or scheme of things that are and that
are to come.

The aforementioned is very important, and it was stressed before the disciples. Jesus was going away, and it was important that they knew the importance of knowing the Anointing. They were to come to *know the Anointing* as the One that sustains, provides, and the power of God in them for ministry. *Christ wanted them to know the Anointing as God's will for them in life and the wisdom to accomplish that life-goal successfully.*

I will resolve this section by saying that our knowledge determines our immortality; the Prophet Hosea, under the auspices of the Holy Ghost stated, "My people are destroyed for lack of knowledge..." Therefore, the more you know, the more you grow, grow in the things of God, grow in the things of eternal life. Your immortality rate increases, and chances of survival more bright.

This type of life ensures success; knowing the Holy Spirit, His Anointing comes alongside us and helps us, and works with us, insuring our outcome through His leading and intervention. And thus, we know that everything will work out okay because we are a part of God's plan, and regardless of how small it appears, it has a part in the big picture and scheme of things, God's will. What is most important is that by His Spirit, we know our part (Romans 8:14, 16-17, 26-28, 2 Corinthians 4:18, 5:7).

Everything the Father Has Is Mine

The Holy Spirit will reveal all that the Father possesses because this is the purpose of His presence in you and me as believers, to reveal that which the Father has given unto His Son. He revealed Himself unto Jesus, no doubt, through His meditation of the scriptures and through fellowship of the Father through prayer and fasting (Matthew 4:1-2). In return, the Father revealed His wisdom to Jesus (John 5:17-31, 32). This wisdom became knowledge that Jesus applied in His earthly ministry, and through the consistent growth in these things, He developed a strong living relationship with the Anointing.

It is paramount to note the following: the Anointing was God's ability to work through Jesus, who was *a legal agent* in the earth (Acts 10:38). He, Jesus, was *very man by birth*, as well as He was *very God* in flesh *through the Anointing* (Philippians 2:5-8). In His earthly ministry, as a result of His fellowship with God's Spirit, the Anointing, *He was a man doing things only God can do on flesh that God anoints, and was doing it through flesh anointed by and inhabited by him in the person of Jesus in earth as a legal agent* (he came through *the womb* of a virgin).

Jesus, through this relationship, was able to understand God's wisdom and also the understanding of how to apply it and was able to *determine accurately* what would come to pass as a result of *the Truth that was in him*. The disciples would also begin to realize this when the Anointing became available to them to host in their own lives. The Anointing of God in and upon the disciples for the purpose of sustaining and to equipping them for ministry, just as he had equipped Jesus with the Anointing for His earthly ministry:

> ...I still have many things to tell you, but you can't handle them now. But when *the Friend (the Comforter, Teacher, Intercessor, Revelator and Advocate)* comes, the Spirit of Truth, He will take you by the hand and guide you into all the truth there is. He won't draw attention to himself, but will make sense out of what is about to happen and, indeed, out of all that I have done and said...Everything the Father has is also mine. That is why I've said, "He takes from me and delivers to you"...
>
> John 16:12-15 (MSG)

In the above passage, we see Jesus and the Anointing, *the comforter*, had a plan. This plan was later to be revealed in the disciples, and Jesus implied that in the following verses of the above passage ([*4]John 16:23-33). The disciples would know all things because all there

---

4 See the MSG or AMP

was to know begins in Him (Jesus Christ, the Anointed). They knew He (Jesus) was from God because God, through His Anointing, so evidently worked with and through Him. They begin to understand that if they follow His footsteps, take on His lifestyle, and pattern their lives after Him, they would come to know the Anointing as Jesus knew Him (the Anointing of the Anointed). The disciples would evolve into effective *legal agents in the earth* in which the Holy Spirit could abide and carry out *His mandate*.

Jesus, although he had not in fact performed the ultimate sacrifice, he already knew the outcome because of the Truth, *Wisdom of God*. The Anointing revealed *the mandate* unto Him (Jesus). He would pay the ultimate price in order that the disciples would be able to realize the same experience of the Anointing.

But, also through these newly *anointed ministers*, others would become believers and would come to know the Anointing through the lives of these *anointed ministers* sharing *the message of the Anointed and His Anointing* (the Gospel of the Kingdom). Jesus would, in fact, conquer through *the Anointing now, abiding upon, living within, and working through them*, as it had performed in Jesus. This was Jesus' prayer concerning the disciples as well as the church that would be established through them (John chapter 17).

CHAPTER 6

The Mandate of Purpose

Purpose Revealed

I believe it's important to make this statement, *realize that life is not a chance but a challenge.* Many of us go through life without purpose. Some wonder aimlessly through life without direction, without goals. And yet, some may have goals or desires but can't realize them for lack of knowledge, direction, and/or the discipline necessary to obtain them. This is the key reason the Word of God is so important to the believer.

Without God and His Word in our life, we will never realize our full potential. We may accomplish some success but never realize the full potential without the involvement and participation of God. *Every man on earth has a purpose,* but until that man meets the *one who originates purpose,* he will never come to fully know true purpose, that is, to find his true direction and goal in life.

Notice I said, "goal in life." At the risk of being somewhat rhetorical, *all life originates out of Creator God*; He declares the end from the beginning (Isaiah 46:10). That means *He knows and declares the outcome* of everything and goes back to the beginning of the thing and *begins the beginning* of the thing. Let me state it another way: He said *I am the Alpha (The Beginning or Author) and Omega (The Ending, Finisher or full development) of a Thing,*

> I am Alpha and Omega, the beginning and the ending, saith the Lord, which is, and which was, and which is to come, the Almighty.
>
> Revelation 1:8

The "Past, Present, and Future" are *presently* before Him. There is no beginning to God because "beginning" connotes a period in time, and *God is outside of time; He resides in eternity.* In fact, *time is an interruption or pause in eternity, to give man "time" to recover from the fall (of Adam), and to catch up with his Creator spiritually.* In other words, God paused a moment and began the beginning[s] or time[s] *out of Himself,* having *known the outcome* and purpose of it in His heart before He began the beginning of it.

This alone should reveal to us how important it is for man to begin with God, who is *the Originator of all things*. God is the light (purpose of your being) of all men. To be without God is to be without light, and consequently, you are in darkness (or without the reason for your being); you are blind to purpose. Note the following in John chapter one:

> The Word was first [5][God's purpose for life]*, the Word present to God [within His Heart, known to Him from beginning to end], God present to the Word [They were one in the same; a mere reflection, because], The Word was God, in readiness for God from day one [to begin destiny out of Himself, the embodiment of His Heart].
>
> Everything was created through Him [Its purpose was already known before He began]. Nothing! Not one thing! Came into being without Him [*first defining its purpose and destiny already established in His heart*].
>
> *What came into existence was Life [an image of Himself, as to His purpose and will for all things He created], and the Life was Light [the knowledge of that purpose and the anointing to accomplish and]* to live by.

---

5 Bracketed comments in the **MSG Translation** are those of the author

The Life-Light [The Glory of His image, The Anointing illuminated that is dissipated the dark or] blazed out of the darkness; the darkness couldn't [overcome or] put it out.

John 1:1-5 MSG (E)

If we know or possess the light, then we possess our purpose in life, which in turn determines our goal in life. Let me say it another way, *our purpose in life determines our goal in life.*

Jesus Learned His Purpose

...yet *learned* he [Jesus] obedience by the things which he suffered...

Hebrews 5:8[b] (E)

I am about to state some strange things that are difficult for *the religious mind* to attain, simply because of *lack of fellowship* with the one who is *the author of all things.* Often when we read the above passage, we accept that He suffered many things in His earthly ministry; the Bible gives sometimes-vivid accounts of them. However, my question to you is, how many of you asked, "What did it take for Him to develop Himself to this point, to begin this ministry knowing full well the outcome in His heart?" If we asked that question, many of us have religiously brushed it off with "well, He is the Son of God." This is true, but if you are a Christian and believe the Word, the Word refers to us also as "sons of God":

> 14 For as many as are *led by the Spirit of God, they are the sons of God.* 15 For ye have not received the spirit of bondage again to fear; but ye have received *the Spirit of adoption, whereby we cry, Abba, Father.* 16 *The Spirit itself [Himself] beareth witness with our spirit, that we are the children of God:* 17 *And if children, then heirs; heirs of God, and joint-heirs with Christ [the Anointed and His Anointing];* if so be that we suffer with him, that we may be also glorified together.
>
> Romans 8:14[b] (E)

Jesus began His ministry at thirty years of age. What took place during the previous twenty-nine years of His life? We know He was born (Matthew 1:18-25, Luke 2:1-20). We have an account of it, along with a few brief years between approximately one and three years of age (Matthew 2:1-16). And we have a brief insight into what His life may have been like at twelve years of age (Luke 2:41-52). But we have very little information beyond that point, up to his adult age of thirty, when He began His ministry (Luke 4:14-19).

What took place in the first twenty-nine years of His life that help Him to find His goal and purpose in life? I want us to go behind the scenes. The passages regarding His life prior to His ministry are informative but not as revealing as we would desire. *Maybe this is because the witnesses never thought that the readers would lose sight of what molds an individual into a moral, sound, and focused contributor to society and the world.* Perhaps they felt that to be too detailed and would be redundant and unnecessary.

Thus, the scriptures in these areas were not descriptive. They did not reveal how no doubt His mother Mary and His father Joseph told Him of His birth, the *Unique and Immaculate Conception* that He was (born of a virgin; Isaiah 7:14). No doubt, Mary told Him of the awesome encounter she experienced when the angel of the Lord visited her (Luke 1:26-38). The angel of the Lord informed her of how blessed she was to have been *selected and favored of God*, to give birth to *His only begotten Son* (Luke 1:26-33). In addition, how the angel described the conception: "The Holy Ghost shall come upon thee, and...over shadow thee...that holy thing...shall be born of thee shall be called the Son of God..." (Luke 1:34-35).

I am sure in my own heart that when he read the scriptures that *He knew that He was reading about Himself, He realized what every believer must realize, and that is, we must see ourselves in the scriptures also.* As born-again

Christians, *we are a new creation, born of the Word of God.*
Yes, no doubt when He was reading what we commonly
refer to as Isaiah 9:6-7, He came to know that they spoke
of Him, He would one day read them with a greater insight than any Jew on the face of the earth. In addition,
possibly, for that very moment, for the first time, He
saw Himself in the scriptures, Saviour of the World.

Imagine, if you will, the young Jesus playing with
John, His first-cousin, and John no doubt becoming
frustrated with Jesus' continual desire to have him
(John) pretend He was nailing Him (Jesus) to the cross.
Why play this way? Maybe because in a child's way, He
saw Himself as a *Champion [Messiah],* very much like
when we played *Superman* or some other *Superhero* as
children.

With the continual rehearsing of His birth from
His parents and within Himself, the continual hearing
of the preaching and reading of the scriptures of the
coming Messiah in the temple, and even the convers-
ing of the scriptures with the elders, something took
place within Jesus. *Truth became illuminated within Him*
just like it must take place in any other individual. *He
became the Word, speaking the Word, Anointed by the Holy
Ghost.*

Yes, He acknowledged that He was God's anointed prophesied in the scriptures, but although it was
prophesied in the scriptures, He still had to *become what*

was prophesied just like we had to become sons of God *through faith in Him and faith in His name.* Remember, *faith is a way of life, not a mode you go into. Jesus had to become this Word of prophecy.* He had *to take on the Word and allow it to become His life and destiny.*

He had to become this Word by faith in that Word and by faith in the God that spoke it through men anointed of Him. He had to believe *He was the Word in the flesh. The very out-shining, manifested Word embodied in the flesh of man so that He could die as a man in man's place.* This did not happen overnight; it took *twenty-nine years of preparation and application,* the same way it takes for us to realize our purpose and calling in God. This experience is what *translates us from children of God to sons of God.*

James, the brother (or *half-brother,* as some would declare according to the flesh) of Jesus had a first-hand account of this and with conviction wrote of it in his letter to the Church:

> 22 But be ye doers [live by application what you see] of the word, and not hearers only, deceiving your own selves [by not applying the Word as a lifestyle]. 23 For if any be a hearer of the word [that is in one ear and out the other], and not a doer [one who acts upon what he hears], he is like unto a man beholding his natural face in a glass [mirror]: 24 For he be-

holdeth himself, and goeth his way [or walks away], and straightway [or moments later] forgetteth what manner of man he was [or he should be or emulate]. 25 But whoso looketh into the [mirror of the] perfect law of liberty [the Word], and continueth *therein* [apply it as a way of life and discipline], he being not a forgetful hearer [because he cannot forget what he lives], but a doer of the work [by application, thus becoming], this man shall be blessed [prosper according to the Word] in his deed [actions, and it's in legal writing].

James 1:22-25

This is the way Jesus lived. *He became what he read through application and lifestyle.* Therefore when He spoke, He spoke with conviction because He was what He preached, *"The Word"incarnate.*

The Right Mental Attitude

The attitude in which we face life or purpose determines our outcome. Our attitude is developed through what is before us most. King Solomon said it like this:

20 My son, attend to my words; incline thine ear unto my sayings. 21 *Let them not depart from thine eyes;* keep them in the midst of thine

heart. 22 For they are life unto those that find them, and health to all their flesh. 23 *Keep thy heart with all diligence; for out of it are the issues [forces] of life.*

Proverbs 4:20-23 (E)

So you see, we must keep those things before us that will enable us to obtain the prize. If you have no hope, you have no goal. For you see, "hope" in the Word of God *has nothing to do with future*, but rather "favorable earnest expectation." "Hope" really implies *you see something (in the spirit, not future)*, that others in most cases, do not see. Let me state it another way, you see spiritually your hope (vision) coming into view, and *since you see it, it is not future* because the spirit realm exists outside of *time*, the natural realm. Note Romans 8:23-25:

23 And not only this, but we too, who have the first fruits of the Spirit [a joyful indication of the blessings to come], even we groan inwardly, as we wait eagerly for [the sign of] our adoption as sons—the redemption *and* transformation of our body [at the resurrection]. 24 For in this hope we were saved [by faith]. But hope [the object of] which is seen is not hope. For who hopes for what he already sees? 25 But if we hope for what we do not

see, we wait eagerly for it with patience *and* composure.

(AMP)

The Word of God paints a picture of hope (success) in your heart that will encourage you to pursue diligently the goal set before you:

> 1 Wherefore *seeing we also are compassed about with so great a cloud of witnesses,* [the scriptures have recorded] let us lay aside every weight, and the sin which doth so easily beset *us,* and let us run with patience *the race that is set before us [the image the word has revealed],* 2 looking unto Jesus the author and finisher of our faith; who for *the joy [the conviction of his hope revealed] that was set before him* endured the cross, despising the shame, and is set down at the right hand of the throne of God. 3 For consider him that endured such contradiction of sinners against himself, lest ye be wearied and faint in your minds.
>
> Hebrews 12:1-3 (E)

God also placed a vision in Joshua's heart (Joshua 1:3-4):

3 Every place that the sole of your foot shall tread upon, that have I given unto you, as I said unto Moses. 4 From the wilderness and this Lebanon even unto the great river, the river Euphrates, all the land of the Hittites, and unto the great sea toward the going down of the sun, shall be your coast.

God informed Joshua that from this point on in your life, every place, the soles of your feet cover would become yours. Wow! What a vision, God was literally saying, the sooner you get busy about learning how to conquer this land, the sooner you will possess it. And, the more of it you will possess, from the rising of the Sun until the going down of the same, as far as the eye can see. Therefore, take it in, and feed the *vision of your heart*, so shall it be with you, Joshua. *That is powerful stuff.*

God also informed him that He would always be there for him, He would never forsake him (Joshua 1:5). In the words of a mentor of mine, *"God never gives a vision without the 'pro'-vision. And God is the provider of every provision to support the vision in your heart provided by Him".*

All things being said and believed, this sets the tone in Joshua's heart for the right mental attitude. Now in order for Joshua to obtain *the right mental attitude*, note what God says to Joshua:

6 Be strong and of a good courage; for unto this people shalt thou divide for an inheritance the land, which I sware unto their fathers to give them. *7 Only be thou strong and very coura-geous, that thou mayest observe to do according to all the law, which Moses my servant commanded thee: turn not from it* to the right hand or to the left, *that thou mayest prosper whithersoever thou goest. 8 This book of the law shall not depart out of thy mouth; but thou shalt meditate therein day and night, that thou mayest observe to do accord-ing to all that is written therein: for then thou shalt make thy way prosperous, and then thou shalt have good success. Have not I commanded thee? Be strong and of a good courage; be not afraid, neither be thou dismayed: for the Lord thy God is with thee whithersoever thou goest.*

Joshua 1:6-9 (E)

When God gives a vision, He stands with you; *He is your source* to everything you need to bring it about. God told Joshua, "Be strong and courageous" (verse 6), and again he said, "Only be thou strong and very coura-geous" (verse 7). Why? Because when you move out in God, you must be focused and *know in your heart that if He called you, He also qualified you* (Philippians 1:6, 4:13).

Joshua learned how to be a leader by observing Moses, his relationship before God and before man.

Paul, no doubt had this in mind when he addressed the church in Rome, writing:

> 2 And be not conformed to this world [its customs and superficial concerns]: but *be ye transformed* by the *renewing of your mind [be changed in your thinking entirely with a new attitude developed by this new life of new ideals], that ye may prove [to yourself and to the world] what is that good, and acceptable, and perfect, will of God [for you].* 3 For I say, through the grace given unto me, to every man that is among you, not to think of himself more highly than he ought to think[do not have an inflated opinion of your on importance]; *but to think soberly [be sound in your judgment of yourself, live within the ability of your faith but demand its continued development to meet the challenge], according as God hath dealt to every man the measure of faith [for we all begin with the same measure of faith but it is up to the believer to develop it for the task at hand].*
>
> Romans 12:2-3 (E)

When you are focused on the Word, you are focused on the Anointing. God informed Joshua to remain focused on the Word, the Vision, the issues of life, and success. Jesus is quoted as saying, "But Seek ye first the Kingdom of God, and His righteousness" (Matthew 6:33[a]).

God instructs the believer to "do first things first...; develop a life submitted to God, a life where God reigns in a man. A life pleasing to God, thus receiving the right of access or the right to approach God in good favor... and all these things [the wisdom to pursue visions, purposes and goals] will be added unto you" (Romans 5:1-5, Matthew 6:33[b], Hebrews 4:14-16).

John the divine states in 1 John 2:20:

> 20 But ye have an unction [an anointing; that knows all things] from the Holy one, and [because He knows all things and is in you] you know all things [the Knower] is resident within you and you have access to all He knows].

The following passage supports the expressions of clarification I added to the above scripture:

> 27 But the Anointing [that unction] which you have received of Him [the Anointed One] abideth...[has residence] in you, and [as a result] you need not that any man [or you need not seek spiritual wisdom or the Anointed's

purpose for you from flesh and blood or] teach you [His purpose for you, which is already within you]: but as the same anointing teacheth [as He is teaching] you of all things, and [because He] is truth, and is no lie [there is no lie in Him, nor any part of Him], and even as it [He] hath taught you [or as you mature in His knowledge of Him] ye shall abide [live conscious of his presence, confident that He is there for you and in and upon you, and you] in Him.

1 John 2:27

The right mental attitude is very important; *the Word* helps us to develop that *right mental attitude*. When you *possess the right mental attitude*, you will not allow anything to deter you from your goal, not people, demons, or devils. With violence, spiritually speaking, if necessary, you will seize what is rightfully yours (Matthew 11:12); however, the kingdom of darkness has no defense against the will of God in you, the believer (Matthew 16:17-18).

I recall the two blind men who believed Jesus to be the Messiah *(the one promised to deliver His people)*; it is recorded in Matthew 9:27: "Thou Son of David, have mercy upon us..." They followed Jesus into His house; no doubt determined to receive what they believe were *theirs by covenant right.* Jesus replied, "Believe ye that I am able to do this [or do you believe that I can do this]?" They replied, "yea Lord." Then He touched their eyes saying, "Become what you believe" (MSG Translation).

The right mental attitude (Romans 12:2) determined *the parameters of their faith,* and *faith gave substance to what they believed,* and Jesus operated within those parameters generated by the right mental attitude developed by the covenant Word of God.

I'm sure you have heard stated the adage, *your attitude determines your altitude.* Well, I want to play on that adage, *your faith attitude determines your faith altitude, limits (or parameters) in which the Anointing operates in your life.* Paul's faith set wide parameters for the anointing, "I can do all things through the anointing which strengthens [develops, equips and qualifies] me." You do the same and become the parameters of the Word, God's ability in you:

> 21 And being *fully persuaded* that, what *He had promised, He was able also to perform.* 22 And therefore it was imputed to him for righteousness. 23 *Now it was not written for his sake alone,* that it was imputed to Him; 24 *But for us also,* to whom it shall be imputed, *if we believe on him* that raised up Jesus our Lord from the dead.

Romans 4:21-24 (E)

When we become *fully persuaded* in the promises of God, no demon, devil, or man, nor any other creature shall be able, or cannot stop us from pursuing our *mandate from God* because our *faith parameters*, developed through the *right mental attitude*, will give *substance* to the *overcoming power to obtain our purpose*, the Anointing will produce it (Romans 8:26-39).

Know the Outcome to Every Challenge

If we realize that every challenge that comes or faces us will come to pass, our outlook is more positive as we face them. For God Himself declared, *"I declared the end from the beginning,...*My counsel [purpose/Word] shall stand, and I will do [perform] all my pleasure [purposes]...yea, I have spoken it, I will also bring it to pass, *I have [planned and] purposed it, I will also do [perform] it"* (Isaiah 46:10-11).

I will not leave anything to assumption. Let me state it in another way, everything we face in life, both positive and especially negative must *first, come,* and *then second, pass away.* If you recall, when you read the scriptures, all of God's patriots faced challenges, and in most cases, the account began with *"And it came to pass."*

Many of us, when reading those particular phrases, assumed it was stated that way because it was something of the past and not the present, or *"Once upon a time,"* God's Word is not a *"fairy-tale,"* it is *"The Book of Truth." The Word states truth* from the perspective as if *you are there,* or *were there* confirming and knowing the challenges that faced the patriots, knowing *first, it came,* and then, *secondly, it passed away (i.e., "...and it came to pass...").*

Might I remind you that *the Word of God is not a history book?* Although the Word has history within it, it is there only as *a point of reference* and not for historical purpose or content. The Word possesses *the Promises of God concerning you:* "I will never leave you or forsake you, I am with you alway" (Matthew 28:20). The word "alway" in the previous quote of Matthew 28:20 is singular because there are *"no ways"* He (God) is not with you. To state the word (alway) in the plural form would imply there are some *"ways"* God would not be with you. Therefore it is correct to state it as translated. That means when you are *right,* He (God) is with you; when you have missed it, God is with you in that situation also. This is *God's promise to us:* "I am with you alway [everywhere, and in every situation]." God is, *in every place and every situation* (Omni-Present). This scripture promise implies that whatever you face in life, I am whatever you need in the midst of it. *I am your all, in all* [situations]. He says, " fear not, for I will uphold you with the right hand of my righteousness" (Isaiah 41:10). David expressed it this way:

> 7 Whither shall I go from thy spirit? or whither shall I flee from thy presence?
> 8 If I ascend up into heaven, thou art there: if I make my bed in hell, behold, thou *art there*. 9 *If* I take the wings of the morning, *and* dwell in the uttermost parts of the sea;
> 10 even there shall thy hand lead me, and thy right hand shall hold me.
> 11 If I say, Surely the darkness shall cover me; even the night shall be light about me.
> 12 Yea, the darkness hideth not from thee; but the night shineth as the day: the darkness and the light *are* both alike *to thee*.
>
> Psalm 139:8

Based on the above, we should have confidence that there is no situation the presence of God, through His Anointing, will not be present to enable us to succeed and fulfill purpose in one's life. Literally, He says anything seen or perceived by the senses is bound to change, especially when it is not in your favor (2 Corinthians 4:18). When you know the outcome of a thing and the outcome is in your favor, you have nothing to fear; simply do your part, and the Anointing will do the rest. His part is honoring your faith in Him through the situation.

Note Isaiah 40:28-31:

> 28 Hast thou not known? hast thou not heard, *that* the everlasting [eternally ever present] God, the LORD, the Creator of the ends of the earth, fainteth not, neither is weary? *there is* no searching of his understanding.
>
> 29 He giveth power to the faint; and to *them that have* no might he increaseth strength.
>
> 30 Even the youths shall faint [resting in their own strength] and be weary [and become faithless],
>
> and the young men shall utterly fall [trusting in their own abilities and wisdom]:
>
> 31 but they that wait [grow like a string into a cord or rope trusting in the anointing;] upon the [wisdom of the] LORD shall renew *their* strength [energize by the anointing]; they shall mount up with wings as eagles [soar with eyes of an eagle over the wiles or oppositions of the enemy]; they shall run, *and* not be weary; and they shall walk, and not faint [with full confidence and faith in God].
>
> (E)

Therefore it is imperative that you know the Word so that you *will not faint* in the day of adversity or *opposition from the enemy*. Proverbs 24:10 says, "...If thou faint in the day of adversity, thy strength [faith] is small..." You will *know the outcome if you SUBMIT yourself to God, first* (James 4:5), that is giving *God's Word first place in your life*, and become *the Word re-incarnate. The enemy must flee from the Anointing of the Anointed One in you, giving you the appearance before the world the image of "sweatless" (or effortless) victory.*

Remember, our confidence is *faith in the Word* "knowing." "Hast thou not known?" (Isaiah 40:28[a]); knowing our outcome will be as the Word declares, "our victory....For this commandment which I command thee this day, it is not hidden from thee, neither is it far off... But the Word is very nigh unto thee, in thy mouth [as the Anointing], and in thy heart [as the Anointed], that thou mayest do [perform] it [your victory/purpose in life]" (Deuteronomy 30:11-14).

The Choice Is Yours

God gives us the choice of success or failure. Choose the Spirit Life, the Anointing, and His Anointed (life) and *reap the blessing*, a success-filled life. To choose contrary to life is to choose death (anti-anointing), a life contrary to the Anointing and *reaping the curse*, a life of failure. In Christ, Success is *inevitable*; failure is *a choice*.

Now keep in mind that "in Christ" declares that your choice is life and everything that ensures it, as a believer. Better yet, you are *one that has become what you believe [or in full confidence]* of the Covenant promise. God declares that we walk within *His pattern for life* (the anointed life) and all that pertains to it is ours. *Any choice outside of it (the Anointed life) is death* (Deuteronomy 30:15-20). *Anyone in the light* (possessing knowledge and confidence in the truth) *chooses life.* The Anointed One has paid the price that we might live the anointed life, the Anointed life, and whosoever that calls upon the name of the Lord (declares Jesus is Lord and His salvation), becomes *a legal recipient of that life.*

Choosing life is choosing victory. "This is the victory that overcomes the world, *our faith* [in the Anointed and His Anointing]" (1 John 5:7). This is the peace that surpasses all understanding, a life living submitted to the Anointing, living *the Anointed life* (Philippians 4:6-9). This Anointed life is a life of confidence in Him who will never leave or forsake us; He is developing in us that life that overcomes every obstacle (James 1:2-4, Philippians 1:28, note the AMP also).

CHAPTER 7

The Holy Spirit Reveals Faith and Hope

For the sake of review, I believe it important that I refresh your mind that the Word "Anointing" is interchangeable with the words *Holy Spirit or Holy Ghost, as well as the words power, life, light, and peace* (in relation to God).

The Anointing Reveals Faith and Hope

With the above in mind, I state the following: some of the major mandates of the Anointing are to *reveal Faith, through His Grace, and Hope.* Note the passages in Romans 5:1-5:

> 1 Therefore being justified [exonerated, vindicated; placed in right standing with God]

by [or through] faith, we have peace, with God through our Lord Jesus Christ [the Anointed and His Anointing]. 2 By whom also we have access by [through] faith into this grace [that is all of God's favor, expressed through the power of His Anointing and His willingness to use that power; His Anointing in our behalf], wherein (or in which) we stand, and [we] rejoice in the hope [as a goal of earnest expectation through the experience) of the glory of [all that He is in us as an Anointed of] God. 3 And not only [this], but [more than this] we glory [that is we exult our God in triumph as an Anointed of His] in tribulations also: knowing that tribulation worketh [develops in us] patience [the ability to be continually, consistently constant regardless to the situation]. 4 And [that type of] patience, [develops an] experience [of an ever increasing faith life]; and [that type of] experience [develops] hope [an earnest expectation that reveals the supernatural vision of God's hope in our hearts]. 5 And [that type of] hope maketh not ashamed [or never disappoints or shames us]; because the love of God is shed abroad in [dispersed or injected into] our hearts by the Holy Ghost [in the Person of the

Anointing] which is given unto us [or in behalf of us].

(E)

The Holy Spirit (The Anointing) Has Been Given To Us

The Holy Spirit is given unto us to reveal God's love
toward us through the revelation of faith and hope in
order to receive His righteousness.

We see that the Anointing is responsible *for revealing faith, hope, and purpose,* and how essential they are
to realize the purpose of God in our life. For instance,
Righteousness can in no way be experienced through feelings,
within our senses or emotions. Righteousness can only
be *realized through faith in Jesus Christ* and His finished
work (The Anointed and His Anointing). Though you
live a hundred lifetimes, you will never *feel* righteous.
We are Justified, exonerated, or in right standing with
God *through faith* in The Anointed and His Anointing.

We can never accept the fact we are born of God and
called of God *except through faith in Him.* We can never accept His purpose for our lives *except through faith*
(Hebrews 11:6). This faith reveals God's love toward us
and introduces the hope of God, *which also becomes our
hope* (Ephesians 1:16-18[a], Romans 5:1-5). *His hope in us
reveals His confidence in us, the redeemed, the object of His
love.* Thus we are encouraged and never disappointed

concerning our ability to do all things through His Anointing (Philippians 4:13). That Anointing enables us *through His presence upon and within us* to go about *doing good and healing all that are oppressed of the devil* because we know that by the revealed faith and hope of His presence in us, He is with us to bring about His purpose (Acts 10:38). A world redeemed. Praise God!

Boldness and Identity through the Anointing

Before we proceed with the topic of Boldness and Identity, we must first understand what the Word *"boldness"* means in the King James translation. *Boldness is an old English word; it means by definition "confidence." Confidence as a result of what is earnestly anticipated unashamedly.*

What can produce this type of "Boldness or confidence"? The Anointing of the Anointed-One; note the passage found in 2 Corinthians 3:12-15:

> 12 Seeing then that we have such hope [earnest expectation, concerning the benefits of the New Covenant] we use great plainness of speech [we speak boldly, hold back nothing, because we have nothing to hide; we want it (the purpose of the Anointing) known]: 13 And not [or nor do we conduct ourselves] as Mo-

ses, which put a veil over his face [to hide the fading of the glory he experienced from being in the presence of God's glory], [so] that the children of Israel could not steadfastly look [or clearly see its fading away, thus realizing a need for a better covenant] to the end [or purpose of that which is abolished [or done away with through the new covenant] 14 But their minds were blinded: for until this day remaineth the same veil [of spiritual blindness upon their minds and hearts] untaken [unremoved] away in the reading of the old testament [covenant]; which veil *[of spiritual blindness]* is done away in Christ [through the Anointing]. 15 But even unto this day, when Moses is read, the veil [of spiritual blindness] is upon their heart.

(E)

The people of Israel were not able to see that the *Old Covenant* was enforced in its day, only to serve until *a better Covenant* become established; the *old one* would be *ratified* with a *new one, A New Covenant* that would maintain the *continual presence and glory of God* upon and within us. Israel was not able to understand this because their *minds were blinded through the law of sin* (Romans 7:22-25; 2 Corinthians 3:14-15).

Jesus came to *abolish the curse of the law*, enabling us to choose life and *live within the law of the Spirit of Life through the Anointing*. For what the old law (covenant) could not do, was *made possible through the new* (Romans 8:1-4).

We continue with 2 Corinthians 3:16-18:

16 Nevertheless when it [or anyone] shall turn [through repentance] to the Lord [and His Anointing], the veil [which hid] shall be taken [or will be done] away [with by the Anointing]. 17 Now the Lord is that Spirit [the One that possesses that Anointing] and where the Spirit of the Lord [or His Anointing] is, there is liberty [burdens are removed and yokes destroyed (Isaiah 61:1-2; 10:27, Luke 4:18-19)]. 18 But we all [who have received the anointing and live under His new covenant], with open face [as unveiled faces and eyes wide open to see and understand through continued meditation of the Word see] beholding as [or like looking] in a glass the glory [that is the presence, splendor and experience of the Anointing] of the Lord [on and in our lives and] are [continually] changed into the same [splendor and] image [as the Anointed in an ever increasing faith] from [one degree of] glory [to

another or]to glory, even as by [or through]
the Spirit of the Lord [the Anointing].

(E)

The Anointing is that spirit that equips us to walk in confidence and experience God's best. The more we know Him, the more we grow in Him, to the extent that we are like him in every way concerning His earthly ministry and resurrected life. This is true identity in the Anointing. And this is what Paul meant by the resounding phrase, "In Christ." This phrase by no means meant residing in the physical body of the Christ, the Anointed One, *but rather residing in the Anointing. The Anointing in and upon you, having the same fellowship with the Anointing of the Spirit as Christ (the Anointed One)* experienced (Luke 4:18).

This was Apostle Paul's experience that he identified with the Christ (the Anointing), and well should it be for every believer (Galatians 2:20). This experience leaves us with *no desire for compromise* because of the benefits that come with being sold out to the Anointing. The *kingdom of God* implemented *by faith* in the believer's life is *the token* that validates this type of *identity* with the Anointing. We have nothing of which to be ashamed (Romans 1:13-17). God will not deny His Anointing; *His Inner Man* will never disappoint, but rather confirm His Anointing in the believer.

Therefore, we do not have to be deceptive or underhanded in our efforts to reach the lost. We rest in the fact that those desiring the truth will know in their hearts that we are sincere, and they will be open and receptive to the truth we preach honestly and clearly, and it will only be obscure to *those whom wish not to receive it* (Note 2 Corinthians 4:1-6).

Let me state clearly what this truth is: the *Anointing is that truth* or *the light* that God spoke into a dark world in Genesis chapter 1, verse 3, and that light was and is that which is God, available to man, to those who receive Him. In fact, when God said in Genesis chapter 1, verse 3, "Let there be light [Light be]," He in fact was saying, "Let there be a manifestation of myself in the world," or in other words, He said, "Me [Word] be and "Me" [the Anointing] was [present in the world]."

This experience of God in and upon you serves as *a down payment of better things to come* (Ephesians 1:13-14). We are experiencing this *reality* of the Anointing in and upon us while in these *"...earthen vessels..." of earth, we call our bodies, so that beyond a doubt the things that we do under the influence of the Anointing is truly of Him, and not of us* (2 Corinthians 4:6-7). Thus beyond a doubt, the glory will go to God to whom all glory and honor is due and not we the vessels, "for no man can do these miracles...except God be with Him" (John 3:2[b]).

This brings us to *the conviction encouraged by Jesus Himself that what He walked in and possessed belong to the Father, and because God is His Father, what was the Father's was His*. *This is walking in true identity* when our conviction in the Anointing is *the same as the Anointed Jesus,* and when we through *the Righteousness of God* accept His Anointing as equally ours as it is the Anointed Jesus (Note John 16:12-15, and Romans 8:17), our ministry will truly be effective.

We will never walk in our *true potential* until we realize within ourselves, as believers, that *our whole purpose in life* is to become *like him in our purpose and calling,* and that is only possible when we establish *a viable life producing relationship* with the Anointing, the Holy Spirit.

Let's resolve here and now: *we are not going to park where we are.* The Spirit of God in us continues to urge us to move forward in the things of God (2 Timothy 2:15, Philippians 3:11-12, 13-15. 16-21). The Hebrew writer in Hebrews 5:8 through Hebrews 6:3, we are reminded that many times when we should be teachers, as Jesus was in His earthly ministry, we are found lacking in spiritual knowledge and in need of increased knowledge concerning the Wisdom of God. The Hebrew writer implies this is a result of a lack of maturity and self-discipline; we become like children in regards to spiritual things. We instead should be well ahead and far advanced from where we are. So he challenges us to step out from the elementary things of what the Anointing has to offer and move on to more advanced things.

This is the Anointing's whole purpose here with us, *to advance us and develop us into that same image that was and is the Anointed Jesus* (James 1:25).

John the divine had an insight on that when in 1 John 4:17 he states, "because as He [the Anointed through His Anointing] is, so are we in this [present] world."

The Anointing, the Source of the Gift

The Holy Spirit, the Anointing on Jesus, and the Anointing in and on the believer is, *the source of all spiritual gifts*. They are not gifts given to utilize as you desire but as the Anointing desires. This gift I'm referring to is based on a Greek word, *Charismata*, a plural form of *charisma*; it depicts its' origin out of grace, *God's unmerited favor*; it is transferred to the believer for a given purpose based on the need of the given situation to obtain God's purpose in it. That is why it is so important for the believer to learn to be sensitive to the leading of the Holy Spirit so that the proper use and purpose of the Anointing is carried out.

The Apostle Paul states in 1 Corinthians 12:1-7:

1 Now concerning spiritual gifts [matters; the endowments of supernatural energy],

brethren, I would not have [or do not want] you ignorant. 2 Ye know that ye were Gentiles [or heathens; without knowledge of God and His Spiritual endowments], [you were] carried away unto these dumb [speechless] idols, even as ye where led [by every whimsical impulse]. 3 Wherefore [or therefore] I give you [or want you] to understand, that no man speaking by [or under the influence of] the Spirit of God calleth Jesus accursed [or be cursed]: and that no man can say that Jesus is the Lord, but [except by or under the influence of] by the Holy Ghost [The Anointing]. 4 Now there are diversities [distinct varieties] of gifts (charismata, Gk.) [or Spiritual endowments, that distinguishes among us as Christians [or Anointed-Ones like Him], but [they are of] the [that] same Spirit [or Anointing]. 5 And there are differences of administrations, but the same Lord. 6 And there are diversities of operation, but it is the same God which worketh [administer] all in all. 7 But the manifestation of the Spirit is given to every man to profit withal [or benefit all].

(E)

As Jesus, in His earthly ministry, learned obedience through meditation of the Word (considering He was the word incarnate), He disciplined Himself to be sensitive to the Spirit, listening to the instructions and directions of the Holy Spirit. Likewise, the Spirit of God requires the same of us as believers, "For as many as are led by the Spirit [the Anointing], they are the sons of God." Jesus so much as implied this to Nicodemus concerning the Holy Spirit:

> 3...Except a man be born of water [cleansing life-changing power of the word] and of the Spirit [the Anointing], he cannot enter into the kingdom of God [the realm where God reigns as King]... 6 That which is born of the flesh is flesh; and that which is born of the Spirit is spirit [an offspring of God through the Anointing]...8 The wind bloweth where it listeth [or wills], and thou hearest the sound thereof, but canst not tell whence it cometh, and whither [where] it goeth: so is every one that is born of the Spirit [we follow His directions and carry out His will]
>
> John 3:5[b]-8 (E)

Once the Holy Spirit reveals our purpose, he (the Holy Spirit) requires our obedience and self-discipline "through faith and patience [we] inherit what has been promised," trusting in Him to carry it out or *manifest what He has placed in us* before the foundation of the world. Note Hebrews 6:11 through 12:

> 11 And we desire that every one of you do shew the same diligence [consistent determination] to [or in realizing] the full [maturity in your] assurance of hope [earnest expectation] unto the end [of ones purpose in the Anointing]: 12 That ye be not slothful [disinterested, spiritual sluggards], but followers [imitators] of them who through *["the spiritual twins"]; faith and patience* inherit [as legal heirs of the Anointed] the [covenant] promises.
>
> (E)

The Apostle Paul's heart felt prayer for each of us was,

> My little children, of whom I travail in [spiritual labor pains of] birth again [and again] until Christ [The Anointing of the Anointed] be formed [fully developed] in you.
>
> Galatians 4:19 (E)

Grow in the grace of God and allow *His purpose* to be manifested *in you, for you, and through you* to the glory and honor of God (Philippians 2:13).

And Great Grace Was Upon Them

The presence of the Anointing upon the believer is a sure token of his ability to prosper spiritually and naturally. In Acts the 4th chapter, we see the results of God's Anointing upon the people. In verses 33 through 35, it states:

> 33 And with great power gave the apostles witness of the resurrection of the Lord Jesus: and great grace [God's favor, God's power (the Anointing), and God's willingness to demonstrate its presence through signs to confirm it] was upon them all. 34 Neither was there any among them that lacked: for as many as were possessor of lands or houses sold them, and brought the prices of the things that were sold, 35 And laid them down at the apostles' feet: and distribution was made unto every man according as he had need.
> (KJ21) (E)

There were those present at this occasion that observed what was taking place and wanted to experience what they observed, taking place in their lives also. They saw how many prospered. However, there were some that were not quite willing to sell out all and thought that deceiving the church leaders would win them the same favor and blessings they saw taking place in others' lives.

Apostle Peter, aware of this *through the Holy Spirit*, addressed Ananias and his wife concerning this resolve between them (Acts 5:1 through 11). Peter informed them that their scheme was an affront to the Holy Spirit (the Anointing) and not to them, the Elders of the church. They lied to Peter in hopes of receiving the same blessings as the others, but they were not willing to make the same sacrifices. Their hearts were corrupt; *they were deceived by Satan,* that advancement with God and His blessings came through the same schemes they played and used in the world, no doubt to gain what wealth they had earned prior to their encounter with the Christian life.

Another occasion of the ability of the Anointing to prosper the people of God is reflected by Apostle Paul in Ephesians 3:20 through 21 (AMP):

Now to Him Who, by (in consequence of) the [action of His] power...His Anointing; ...that is at work within us, is able to [carry out His purpose]

And one of those purposes is to prosper us;

...[and] do super-abundantly, far over and above all that we [dare] ask or think [infinitely beyond our highest prayers, desires, thoughts, hopes, or dreams]...in Christ [the Anointing of the Anointed] Jesus throughout all generations forever and ever. Amen (so be it).

In Paul's salutation in the same letter (Ephesians 1:3), he states:

Blessed be the God and Father of our Lord Jesus Christ [The Anointed and His Anointing], who *hath* blessed us with all spiritual blessings in heavenly *places [things (provisions)]*.

Let it be known now, do not be deceived. As Apostle James declared, "every good gift and every perfect gift is from above, and cometh down from the Father of lights [which produces your provisions]" (James 1:17).

Those provisions recorded by Apostle Paul in Ephesians 1:3 are of the anointing that will manifest those necessary resources that are stored up for you (in the realm of the spirit) for the purpose He (God) has called you to. Remember, He promised to supply *all your need* (no 's' on the end of "need," God is *all-inclusive*), according to *His riches and glory* by Christ [or through the Anointing of the Anointed] Jesus. *The source of everything we need is in the Anointing.*

Jesus stated, *"if you abide in me [through the Anointing,* maintain a living working relationship with me and my Anointing] and my words *[which are Anointed] abide [take residence and have their place] in you,* ye shall ask [the Anointing, in you and upon you] *what you will [demand],* and [through the anointing in and upon you] *it shall be done [in your behalf]"* (John 15:8).

This is giving glory to God, you producing everything necessary to be fruitful and successful in what He has called you to by the power (His Anointing) that is at work in you and upon you in life.

Our source is in the Anointing. In the Anointing, *the gifts of the spirit* are made available to the believer. There are three categories of gifts revealed in the Anointing, the divine order of manifestation. Those categories are *revelation gifts, power gifts, and vocal gifts* (1 Corinthians 12:4-11). Paul states in the first verse of 1 Corinthians chapter 12, verse 1[b], "I will not have you ignorant..." You see, it is essential to know the Anointing and His many-faceted ways and mandate.

The more we know him (the Anointing), the more we grow in success toward our purpose and calling. The more we know him, the more we can be utilized in his many-faceted ways as he moves and reveals himself to us, the believers.

Paul's heart felt desire was,

> [For my determine purpose is] That I may know [or have (gonosko (Greek)) an intimate (personal) relationship with] him [the Anointing of the Anointed]. [So] That I may become more deeply and intimately acquainted with him. And in that same way come to know the power [or the might of his being] overflowing which he [personally] exerts over the believer...
> Philippians 3:10[a] (AMP) (E)

This explains more clearly what is implied of Paul in 1 Corinthians Chapter 12 in verses 11 through 20. These gifts are given to every believer, "...severally..," [two or more] (verse 11, KJV) as he the Anointing wills. Each member has a distinct part in the move of His purpose that is a benefit to the whole even as the parts of the body are all different with different functions, but they all work in cooperation with each other for the benefit of the whole body.

Now in verses 21 through 31 Paul begins to illustrate there are no big "I's" and little "u's" in the make-up of the body. *All* the parts are *essential*, and *all* the parts *need each other*, and *all* the parts are *mysteriously interwoven* to depend upon each other for the *one body* to *function effectively*. Although each member has a particular and different part to perform within the body, *that difference carried out fully benefits the whole body and places that member in unity (not union) with the whole body.*

Paul, in verse 25 further, reveals that the body was designed this way so that there would be *no division or dissension in the body*. Likewise, the Holy Spirit in his divine administration performs His function in the church according to *the mandate of the God-Head*. The Holy Spirit assigns offices (callings) based on the pre-determined counsel of His own will (Ephesians 1:10-11), His purpose, which is the ability of each individual, to perform the divine will of the anointing. This knowledge is the adhesive bond that holds all this together, *The Love of God*.

This knowledge is *the excellence of God in each of us*. Each of us pursuing his love helps us to perform in *God-like excellence*, and we are available for whatever is needed and necessary at that given time. We are not limited to a specific gift, but under divine control of the Holy Spirit, we can be sufficient for every occasion, for his love never fails (1 Corinthians 13:8).

CHAPTER 8

The Holy Spirit
Reveals Purpose

The *knowledge of the love of God and its implementation in our lives reveals the purpose of the Holy Spirit,* which is to bring *the church* into *Spiritual unity. The mandate of the Holy Spirit* is, *to reveal unity to the earthly family (the church),* a unity that can only be attained through the principle, *the bond of peace* (Ephesians 4:1-3). The bond of peace is God's love which serves as the foundation of God's character (the foundation of the fruit of the spirit (Galatians 5:22-23, Ephesians 5:9-10)).

In Ephesians chapter 4, Paul reveals one of the Holy Spirit's mandates, *the unity of the body of Christ,* and, the underlying element, *or foundation, the love of God.* There would be no church if it were not for *the Person of Love* (1 John 4:7-9 AMP):

7 Beloved, let us [unselfishly] love *and* seek
the best for one another, for love is from God;

and everyone who loves [others] is born of God and knows God [through personal experience]. 8 The one who does not love has not become acquainted with God [does not and never did know Him], *for God is love. [He is the originator of love, and it is an enduring attribute of His nature.]* 9 By this the love of God was displayed in us, in that God has sent His [One and] only begotten Son [the One who is truly unique, *the only One of His kind]* into the world so that we might live through Him.

(E)

God's name is Love; we can literally use "Love" interchangeably between the word "God" and any proper noun that reflects him as principal (i.e., the "Word"), "that whosoever believeth in him [Love]......have everlasting [eternal] life" (John 3:16, KJV). Paul earnestly appeals for us to make it our duty or purpose to *live in unity with the Holy Spirit.* In so doing, we would be in direct *unity with the purpose and mandate of the Holy Spirit* concerning the church and the divine order of God's plan.

Unison Vs. Unity

Take note, by definition, *union and unity are two different things.*

Unison is every part within a group *performing the same function.* Each instrument in an orchestra playing the same pitch is unison.

Unity, on the other hand, is *two or more parts performing separate or different functions within a given group, but both working toward the same goal.* As an example, *unity* would be very similar to a *football team,* each player has a *different position* to play, but each player has *the same goal—to outperform or overcome their opponents, advance, or defend the ball and eventually win the game, as a unified team.*

The Holy Spirit was commissioned to bring the church into *unity, not unison* (Ephesians 4:1-8, 11-16). *Each member of the body doing his part to accomplish the purpose of the head of the body, Jesus the Anointed and His Anointing, the head of the church.* The Holy Spirit, through the anointing, utilizes each of us in the overall divine picture to accomplish *His purpose in the earth, the body (the Church) in unity with the God-Head (through the Anointing) in the divine scheme of things.*

Apostle Paul to the Church in Corinth expressed the importance of the unity of the Church as the body of

Christ. In 1 Corinthians 12:12-14, 18 illustrated this in his analogy of the human body:

12 For as the body is one [the sum of all of its parts], and hath (have or composed of) many members, and all the members [with its different functions] of [or within] that one body, [although] being many [members or parts], are [yet] one body [in purpose and function]: so also [likewise] is [the purpose and function of the] Christ [the Anointing, and His Anointed-one[s]] 13 For by one Spirit are we all baptized [submersed, immersed, absorbed, and consumed of His purpose and will] into one [unique, holy unified spiritual] body,...and have been all made [inundated, engulfed, and overwhelmed] to drink into [partake in this covenant, one for all and all for one; His purpose for us, which we discover is our reason and purpose for being, and we live for it, and are given life by it as we habitually live in the unity of the purpose of His] one [unifying, harmonizing] Spirit. 14 For the body is not one member [unit or single parts performing in unison the same function], but many [independent, vital parts with a unique specific function contributing its part to the whole

body in order to sustain or support the overall existence or purpose of the total body]...18... God [by His predetermined counsel] set [ordered the purpose, function and contribution of each] the members [individually] every one of them in the body, as it hath [has] pleased Him.

(E)

Before proceeding, let me make a qualifying statement that takes us a step further in recognizing the significance of the Holy Spirit as the Third Person of the God-Head; *The Holy Spirit is the presence of God's will and power in the world today. The Anointing is that power in contact with an obedient man or woman of God willing and available to allow the will and power of God to live through him or her.* This is an *essential prerequisite* to understanding and growing in the knowledge of God.

Union In Relation To Unity

The next thing to address is *Union in relation to Unity.* The Church is called to *Unity,* but that can only be accomplished through the Church coming into *Union with Christ;* this is what I call *oneness or true identity* with the finished work of Christ Jesus (Galatians 2:20-21), and what it provides for the believer (Luke 10:17-20, Matthew 28:18-20).

Unity in Relation To Differences

There can be *no unity without respect of differences*. As the body has many members (1 Corinthians 12:1-31), *its function depends upon its unity of each member's assigned purpose,* thus reflecting *the union of the body* to accomplish its *purpose*. Based on the aforementioned, we see where the body functions *in unity* in order to accomplish *the union of the body's purpose or given function*.

Again, there can be *no unity without union*. The *unity of the Church* can only be realized by each member of the Church coming into *union or unified agreement with the Head of the Church, Christ Jesus our Lord*.

The Power of God Is the Gospel

We often think of the Holy Ghost as the power of God when in fact, the power of God is revealed in Romans 1:16:

For I am not ashamed of the gospel [*good news*] of Christ [*The Anointing and His Anointed*]: for it [*the gospel, the good news*] is the power of God

unto salvation to every one that believeth
[*committed to live by this Gospel*]...

(E)

Therefore, *the power of God is the gospel,* the good news
of Christ Jesus, and His Anointing (John 1:1, 14, 5:19,
8:26-29). The Holy Spirit's Anointing and the Anointed Jesus were *simply moving in concert with the will (The
Word, The Gospel) of God,* in His highest sovereignty [El-
Elyon (Hebrew)] (Genesis 14:18-20, Psalm 78:35); note
Mark 16:20:

20 And they [the disciples; believers] went
forth, and preached [the Gospel] every where,
the Lord working with them [in concert], and
confirming the word [preached] with signs
following [spiritual manifestations; comple-
menting the word preached]. Amen.
(E)

What were the signs? Note Acts 8:5-8:

5 Then Philip *[6][a disciple; a follower of
Christ] went down to the city of Samaria,
and preached Christ [the Anointed and His

6 King James translation; words in brackets are the author's for
clarity.

Anointing; the Gospel] unto them.6 And the people with one accord gave heed [listen and observed] unto [in regard to] those things which Philip spake [spoke], hearing and seeing the miracles which he did. 7 For unclean spirits, crying with loud voice, came out of many that were possessed with them: and many taken with palsies, and that were lame, were healed. 8 And there was great joy in that city.

(E)

Philip apparently preached the gospel, the delivering power of *the Anointing, and the Anointing confirmed the Word with signs of deliverance and healings,* and as a result, there was great joy in that city.

Therefore, everything that is God's will comes into play when there is a *qualified willing vessel (Spirit-filled mature Believer) ministering the Gospel,*

> ...for it is the power of God unto salvation to everyone that believeth...
>
> Romans 1:16[b]

Remember:

[Not in your own strength] for it is God [*by His Spirit*] who is all the while effectually at work in you [energizing and creating in you the power and desire], both to will and to do [work] for *his* good pleasure [satisfaction and delight].

Philippians 2:13 (AMPC) (E)

When we come into *unity* with *God's will through faith*, when our faith is "effectually fervent," that is a person whose faith has become intensely energized with a strong desire and delight to please God in his life. Then, we walk into the reality of the aforementioned verses (Romans 1:16 and Philippians 2:13). Our hearts come into *concert with the Will of God; we identify with the faith of God.*

For in the Gospel a righteousness which God ascribes is revealed, both springing from faith and leading to faith [disclosed through the way of faith that arouses to *more faith*]. As it is written, The man who through faith is just and upright shall live *and* shall live by faith [Habakkuk 2:4].

Romans 1:17 (AMP) (E)

When we submit ourselves to God, the Will of God is carried out in accordance to that part (anointing) that is ours, that part according to God's good pleasure. God's good pleasure is the presence of God's Spirit in our spirits and upon our flesh through the Anointing. We do this in concert and in unity with the overall scheme of God's plan and mandate in and through the Church.

Consequently, it is the power of God working through the Believer in concert with the Will of God (The Gospel) that heals the sick, opens the eyes of the blind, causes the lame to walk, and raises the dead, even performs the miracle power of salvation (Romans 1:17). He upholds all things "by the Word of His power" (Hebrews 1:3). However, it is the Anointing of God that reveals the time, place, and purpose in which he desires to perform His power and upon whom He wishes to express Himself in this way (Luke 4:18).

The Word declared that God made known His acts (power) to Israel and His ways unto Moses (Psalm 103:7). This is why some Christians are puzzled when God performs His power through them, and on other occasions, He does not. God refuses to release His power into the hands of individuals that do not know Him (His Word) and His ways (Ephesians 3:10 AMP).

This is an essential element to understanding our part individually and collectively concerning *the mandate of the Anointing.*

God must be able to *trust us with His power* and *His Anointing*. We must be *faithful* to His Will and His purpose for our lives. We must *continually seek His fellowship and abide in His presence*. David declared, "Surely...I will dwell in the house (the presence) of the Lord forever" (Psalm 23:6). Note this passage in Psalm 25:9-10, 12-14:

9 The meek [one who knows the God he is in covenant with, and in whom he knows his strength resides] will he [God] guide in judgment (Righteousness): and the meek [one who knows who he is in covenant with and in whom he knows his strength resides] will he (God) teach his way.

10 All the paths of the Lord *are* mercy and truth unto such as keep his covenant [Word] and his testimonies [sayings]...12...What man *is* he that feareth [reverently respect and worshipful reverence of] the Lord? Him shall he [God] teach in the way [teach His ways] *that* he shall choose [teach him how to choose the best or success]. 13 His soul shall dwell at ease (peace and prosperity); and his seed shall inherit (seize) the [wealth of the] earth. 14 The secret of the Lord [God's plan, that brings these things about] is with them that fear

him; and he will shew [reveal] them [through]
his covenant [Word].

(KJ21) (E)

We must be committed to beginning and ending "In
Him": "Christ in you, the Hope of Glory" (Colossians
1:27[b]). *Do not grieve the Holy Spirit; He is the best friend*
you will ever have. *Desire His presence.* This requires *a*
lifestyle of Prayer and fellowship before our God. It also requires *a fasted life, a life of discipline and restraint,* more
than a life of fasting foods. A fasted life requires or in-
cludes facing some challenges in life that appear to be
difficult to overcome. *Declaring a fast requires faith,* and
entering into the fast *declaring the victory,* and *thanking*
God for the victory while in the midst of the fast, and *not*
closing the fast until the victory is revealed in your heart (Isaiah 58:6-14).

It requires trusting that God will reveal his answer
for you in any given situation through Prayer, praying
in the spirit, and trusting that God will reveal to you,
that is, make your understanding fruitful concerning
your break-through or answer.

Note this passage in 1 Corinthians 2:4-10:

4 And my speech and my preaching was not
with enticing words of man's wisdom, but
in demonstration of the Spirit and of pow-

er: 5 That your faith should not stand in the wisdom of men, but in the power of God. 6 Howbeit we speak wisdom among them that are perfect: yet not the wisdom of this world, nor of the princes of this world, that come to naught: 7 But we speak the wisdom of God in a mystery [hidden plan], even the hidden wisdom, which God ordained before the world unto our glory; 8 Which none of the princes of this world knew: for had they known it, they would not have crucified the Lord of glory. 9 But as it is written, Eye hath not seen, nor ear heard, neither have entered into the heart of man [the un-regenerated], the things which God hath prepared for them that love him [born of His Spirit]. 10 But God hath revealed them unto us by his Spirit; for the Spirit searcheth all things, yea, the deep things of God.

(E)

CHAPTER 9

The Mandate of the Unity of the Church

Jesus Prayed For Unity

The prayer of Jesus, in the Gospel of John, chapter seventeen, is *the Lord's Prayer for the Church*, the body of Christ. However, the church, for the most part, has universally taught Matthew 6:9-13 as *the Lord's Prayer*, when in fact it is a *Prayer Outline* given the disciples and believers who believed Jesus was and is the Messiah (the Anointed). He, Jesus, instructed the disciples to pray in this manner given in Matthew 6:9-13 because as *new covenant* believers, they possess *the legal right* to usher in *the Kingdom of God*. This was God's mandate [hidden plan for the church], for his soon-to-be-established church (the family of God), which they would realize through the fulfillment of Christ's ministry in the earth (Romans 8:12-17).

Furthermore, it should be noted that although Jesus lived under the *Old Covenant, He ministered* the *New Covenant message.*

Although it is not the scope of this composition, the message Jesus preached (the Kingdom of God) expressed *the Kingdom was at hand (now available).* I want to make it clear and understood: Christ did not come to establish the old, but *a new and promised covenant,* God's will for the church composed of born-again believers living under *the kingdom principles.*

Note the following passage:

> 14 Then came to him the disciples of John, saying, Why do we and the Pharisees fast oft, but thy disciples fast not? 15 And Jesus said unto them, Can the children of the bridechamber mourn, as long as the bridegroom is with them? but the days will come, when the bridegroom shall be taken from them, and then shall they fast. 16 No man putteth *a piece of new cloth unto an old garment,* for that which is put in to fill it up taketh from the garment, and the rent is made worse. 17 Neither do men *put new wine into old bottles:* else the *bottles break,* and the *wine runneth out,* and the *bottles*

perish: but they put *new wine into new bottles, and both are preserved.*

Matthew 9:14-17 (E)

The old covenant was a perfect covenant (Romans 8:3-4), but no man could live it except Jesus Christ. He lived it perfectly and then took on your sins (2 Corinthians 5:17-23) to fulfill the old covenant's legal charge against you (Hebrews 9:11-21). Thus, Christ fulfilled and ratified the old covenant as your substitute and obtaining in himself legal authority to establish the new and better covenant of better promises void of any curses (Hebrews 8:6-7).

As born-again believers, *the kingdom principles* would abide within them, thus allowing the believer to live above *the law of sin and death (dominating it through the born-again spirit)*, which the Old covenant was unable to do because it was hindered by the curse and the sinful flesh nature, *the law of sin and death ruling in the flesh.*

However, through *the new birth* of the believer, he or she would live under a new law free of the curse, *the law of life that is in Christ Jesus (the Anointing of the Anointed Jesus).* This new law would enable the believer to live above the curse, thus dominating it, in the flesh through the anointing of God abiding upon and within each believer, his victory resting in the finished work of Jesus Christ.

As the believer grows in the kingdom, he or she will begin to understand *the mandate of the anointing*. The believer, as he grows in the kingdom principles, as sons of God, he or she will begin to realize the importance of being led by and obedient to the Spirit of the living God.

Based on the above, as mature men and women of God, these believers become *the incarnate word, speaking the word, anointed by the Holy Spirit...Christ in you [the church] the hope of glory...*These are believers submitted to the Spirit of God, walking in *the unity of the spirit, through the faith of Jesus Christ, through the bond of peace (the Love of God).*

Now, returning to the original thought, let's address Jesus' prayer in the Gospel of John:

> 4 I have glorified thee on the earth: I have finished the work which thou gavest me to do.
> 5 And now, O Father, glorify thou me with thine own self with the glory which I had with thee before the world was.
>
> John 17:4-5

Here we see Jesus praying and addressing the Father about the position he held in heaven in relation to the Father. He is requesting once again to be *restored* to His former state. *His mandate from Father-God* in the earth was nearing its completion. However, as we see, his concern is now directed to the disciples and the responsibilities that are ahead of them. Note that His answer for their success is The Word:

> 6 I have manifested thy name unto the men which thou gavest me out of the world: thine they were, and thou gavest them me; *and they have kept thy word...8...For I have given unto them the words which thou gavest me; and they have received them...*
>
> John 17:6, 8[a] (E)

Jesus' prayer is an implication to each of us that in order to accomplish the vision of God, *we must be recipients (born) of the anointed Word. The Word of God reveals the Will of God,* but God's will means nothing without *anointed born-again willing and obedient vessels* in which to execute the will of God (Isaiah 1:18-19).

Therefore we see in John 17:22 that the same *glory* that rested upon Jesus to accomplish His goals, which was *the source of the anointing* (Luke 4:18), He gives this glory to His disciples:

> 17 And *the glory which thou gavest me I have given them*; that they may be one, even as we are one:
>
> John 17:22 (E)

His prayer declares that in order for them to be one, in unity, they must have the *Word of unity*, the *same Word* that *made Him one with the Father* in His earthly ministry, through the Anointing:

> I in them, and thou in me, that they may be *made perfect in one...*
>
> John 17:23[a]

Unity That Transcends Differences

In His prayer for the disciples (the Church), He (Christ) requested of the Father that we *may reflect His glory* distinctly *through perfect unity* that transcends *all natural differences* and that we will be perfectly *united in one brotherhood through the Spirit of Love in His Anointing*.

When the Church matures to this *state of unity*, it will *abolish all areas of racism and division* because *perfect love removes all fear of differences* (1 John 4:18).

Differences are not a bad thing; in fact, covenant is built or established upon *differences*. For instance, *God cut covenant with Abram*, God becomes a friend to a man, and that man became a covenant friend with God Almighty, thus what God promised Abram changed him, and through him, a nation was born, the people of God— through Abram who entered the covenant with God and changed his name to testify that he was *a friend of God* and walked in His favor.

Jonathan cut covenant with David, a Prince in covenant with David; a warrior favored of God, the warrior became a symbol of fear to the enemies of the Prince. The Prince became a symbol of royal favor to the warrior.

In the explanations above, *none of the covenant partners had anything in common* with each other, but what each brought to the table, which was *their differences*, became *a strength and access* to the other that, *prior to the covenant, did not exist.* This is far as I will go concerning covenant because it is not the scope of this composition. However, every Christian should study all that he can on covenant because it has such a powerful natural impact on the psyche of a man that enters into one and the conditions that come with *the covenant cut.* The believer should never fear differences because those differences become strength to each covenant partner; *covenant is the foundation of God's Word,* God's covenant with man.

On the other hand, *fear of differences* is what Satan has used to bring down nations. As an example, Satan has used racism as one of his greatest tools of disarming the power of God in the Church and nations. Racism almost divided this nation. Even today, some politicians use it to manipulate and influence the masses to accomplish their goals.

All of us came from *one man (Adam)*. Therefore anything that attempts to implicate *a difference* between men, other than talents, experiences, or any argument contrary to us being of the same species, is *an instrument of witchcraft*. Biblically speaking, the *definition of witchcraft is manipulation*, through the influencing of the will, by means of *familiars [satanic spirits]* who are assigned to you by Satan to *know* you, thus *"familiar spirit"* (Leviticus 19:31).

The human species, and especially those born of the spirit, should never be influenced or motivated through their *emotions*. When an individual is motivated by his or her emotions, *we cease to be rational, but rather irrational*. God never intended for us to be led by our emotions, but rather, our intellect submitted to our spirit (James 4:7). To be rational, one must weigh issues according to knowledge (both spirit and natural (Proverbs 1 (all)).

When one is emotionally driven, we no longer are acting *according to knowledge and intellect* but according to our *feelings*. Human emotions are not designed for discerning *right or wrong; it is no longer the issue* when our emotions are in charge (Proverbs 16:32).

To be emotionally driven is that point where everything is based upon pure selfish, self-centered feelings. Remember this: *emotions void of intellect and knowledge is madness* (Proverbs 15:14, Ecclesiastes 7:25). That is why Apostle Paul stated the following:

16 This I say then, *Walk in the Spirit*, and ye shall not *fulfil the lust of the flesh [you will not become a victim of flesh where the emotions reside].* 17 For the flesh *lusteth [resist by nature]* against the Spirit [human spirit], and the Spirit [human spirit] against the flesh [base nature; lacking or *indicating the lack of* higher qualities of *mind or spirit*]: and these are contrary the one to the other: so that ye *cannot do the things that ye would.* 18 But if ye *be led of the Spirit, ye are not under[or no longer subject to] the law [the law of sin and death].*

Galatians 5:16-18 (E)

God's church can never be driven by our flesh or "self-centered, self-confident or self-nature," for it is *the seat Satan sits upon.* Satan's authority is the realm of the flesh, *the law of sin and death* (Romans 8:1-3). Jesus stated, "ye [you] do error not knowing the scriptures" (Matthew 22:29). Rather we, the church, should be led by the spirit, *God's Spirit upon and within us, the church.* We, the church, must abide in the realm of the spirit, *a higher realm of authority than the realm of the flesh.*

The *authority of the church is living in the spirit*, directed and influenced by the spirit and knowledge of God's Word. The Word of God gives the church the wisdom to know and identify the stratagems of Satan (Ephesians

6:10-18) and how to over through the kingdom of darkness. Remember, the works of the flesh (where Satan
rules) are only defeated through the knowledge of God's
Word and our faith in that Word (1 John 5:4-5); we cannot defeat Satan with just mere human knowledge.

Likewise, we must know the wisdom of man that we
may know them according to their fruit; we are instructed to know (judge) no man according to the flesh or human intellect (Matthew 7:15-20) but according to their
spirits (man's character is revealed by his or her words
and his or her heart). Jesus stated, "for of [out of] the
abundance of the heart his mouth speaketh [speaks],"
the spirit is the window to their soul (Proverbs 20:27, 1
Corinthians 2:15-16, 1 Corinthians 12:4-11, 10). In 1 Corinthians 12:10 it is expressed *the gift of discernment*, a gift
to identify spirits influencing an individual.

Let's conclude: we must never stop educating our
children (our posterity), teaching them both spiritual
knowledge and natural knowledge. Otherwise, we are
doomed to fall. Yes, America, this great nation that was
founded by God-fearing educated men and women.
These men and women, though not perfect, believed
and were taught the Word of God and the history of
mankind. I believe that is why this great nation's leaders were inspired to write such a great Constitution,
a document clearly inspired of God reflecting strong
Judeo-Christian principles, a nation in covenant with God,

so that we would not fall as other nations in the past, which fell as a result of rebelling against God and becoming victims of the sin nature, *the law of sin and death*. When one studies history, you will discover that nations of the past fell as a result of turning from Godly principles and submitted to greed, and perversion in their society, all of which is the works of the flesh (the spirit of darkness).

Remember, however, the only way this nation can fall is that we turn from the living God and stop educating our posterity, of which the result will be, *we are doomed to repeat history*. Keep in mind that ignorance of the law (spiritual and natural) is *the foundation of sin*. The major importance of history is that *we should not repeat it*. We should learn from history, not necessarily repeat it.

Let me state my case this way, *differences* from the standpoint of lifestyles. Let's look at a few of the disciples; they reflect *a type of the church*, all colors, cultures, nationalities, and lifestyles. For example, Peter, a Jew and businessman, a liar with a foul mouth (Matthew 26:69-75), and a bigot (Galatians 2:11-14). Matthew, a tax collector, was considered *an outcast or elitist* by the people, but one of the boys concerning the system of that day (a good old boy). Then, there is Simeon the Canaanite (a black man [Niger], Acts 13:1) and Judas Iscariot, the keeper of the bag (treasurer, John 12:5-6), a thief and betrayer of Jesus (Luke 22:48), Saul (Acts 13:1), soon to be called Paul a well-educated concerning the law (of the Jews) consented to the execution of Stephen, and a persecutor of the early church, a Pharisee by linage; then there is Luke, a physician.

Yet in spite of these flaws in some of their characters, social position, physical appearances, or backgrounds, Jesus loved them through the eyes of faith. He would not allow the attitudes of society or their personal flawed characters stop Him from his mandate *to establish his nation, the church* composed of all nationalities and backgrounds *through faith and love* (1 Corinthians 10:32, 33).

Each of them, all from different backgrounds yet *became one under the message of the gospel* of Christ. Christ Jesus knew that their lives would undergo *super-natural change* through *the new birth* that would be *possible through His death and resurrection.* This would give him *a legal right* to reclaim (redeem) them into a *new covenant of love and unity.*

Christ knew that in them, His church, His nation, His family, and His kingdom, all nations shall be blessed (Genesis12:1-3, Matthew 6:9). He knew that in spite of the ways things look now, a change was going to come, *for the joy* that was set *before Him* He *endured the cross* to insure it (Hebrews12:1-2).

One Nation under God

Jesus knew that we would eventually, through it all, come to realize that regardless to what laid ahead, regardless to what was stored up, regardless to how far our ways were from his ways, that through it all, through the generations of times, we would come to know, we would come to realize how important *love and unity* would be to *the family of God, the Church*. For, after all, this was and is the *Mandate of the Anointing*:

10 That in the dispensation [the stewardship of the Anointing through] the fullness of times he might gather together in one (unity) all things in Christ [The Anointed and His Anointing], both which are in heaven, and which are on earth; even *[particularly]* in him:
11 In whom also we *have obtained an inheritance*, being predestinated according to the purpose of him who worketh all things after the counsel of his own will:

Ephesians 1:10-11

We are a family; we are of the household of faith. Family is the very nucleus of what unity is. There is power in unity. We have held back so many blessings in which God desires to bestow upon us *due to the lack of unity.* And we will not realize these blessings until we begin to love each other and respect each other as brothers and sisters, conscious of our difference but *acknowledging them as strengths* and not handicaps or curses. We are the church, the family of God. In order to hear our God, we must come together as *one in love* and as a family. Note Genesis 48:1-6 (NIV):

> 1 Some time later Joseph was told, "Your father is ill." So he took his two sons Manasseh and Ephraim along with him. 2 When Jacob was told, "Your son Joseph has come to you," Israel rallied his strength and sat up on the bed. 3 Jacob said to Joseph, "God Almighty appeared to me at Luz in the land of Canaan, and there he blessed me 4 and said to me, 'I am going to make you fruitful and increase your numbers. I will make you a community of peoples, and I will give this land as an everlasting possession to your descendants after you.' 5 "Now then, your two sons born to you in Egypt before I came to you here will be reckoned as mine; Ephraim and Manasseh will be mine, just as Reuben and Simeon are mine. 6 Any children born to you after them will be yours; in the territory they inherit they

will be reckoned under the names of their brothers.

God is telling us something here: do you want to obtain your inheritance and know your destiny? *Get together, church!* And hear what your Father has to say, Jesus said in Matthew chapter 18:19:

> 19 Again I say unto you, That if two of you shall *agree on earth* as touching any thing that they shall ask, *it shall be done* for them *of my Father* which is in heaven.

Get together church so that we may obtain our inheritance. The *mandate* is black, white, brown, red, and yellow brothers coming together to hear and fulfill our destiny. It's not about a specific ethnic group coming together or a nation coming together outside of God. That's not God's plan; it's about the church becoming "one." There can be *no unity in the world without God* and *without His Anointing reigning in our life.*

The Anointing is declaring this message in the New Covenant,

> 14 For this cause I bow my knees unto the Father of our lord Jesus Christ, 15 *Of whom the whole family in heaven and earth is named,* 16

That He would grant you,...*to be strengthened with might by His Spirit in the inner man*; 17 *That Christ may dwell in your hearts by faith*; that ye, being rooted and grounded in love, 18 May be able to comprehend with all saints what is the breadth, and length, and depth, and height; 19 And to *know the Love of Christ (the Anointing)*, which passeth knowledge (sense knowledge),...

Ephesians 3:14-19 (E)

1 I therefore, the prisoner of the Lord, beseech you that ye *(the church) walk worthy of the vocation wherewith ye are called*, 2 With all lowliness and meekness, with longsuffering, *forbearing one another in love*; 3 *Endeavoring to keep the unity of the Spirit in the bond of peace.* 4 There is *one body*, and *one Spirit*, even as ye are called in *one hope* of your calling;

Ephesians 4:1-4 (E)

In other words, *a family of unity under or submitted to God* (Philippians 1:27), let's continue in Ephesians 4:5-6:

5 *One Lord, one faith, one baptism*, 6 *One God* and Father of all, who is above all, and through all, *and in you all.*

And if He is "in us all," then His Spirit and Will should be realized in each of us, every one of us should be centered in Him, One Lord, the center and heart of us all: *He is the wheel in the wheel.* Note Christ Jesus in the above scripture passage (vs. five); "One Lord" is the fourth (4th) of seven items (or the *central principle* of the seven) that defines "Spiritual Unity." We must live under these principles by applying them to our lives daily. As we read further (Ephesians 4:7):

> 7...unto every one of us is given grace according to the measure of the gift of Christ [The Anointing]...12....For the perfecting [maturing] of the saints, for the work of the ministry, for the edifying of the body of Christ [The Anointed and His Anointing]; 13...Till we all come in[to] the unity of the faith, and of the knowledge of the Son of God, *unto a perfect [mature Christ centered] man, unto the measure [standards] of the stature [image] of the fulness of Christ [The Anointing]:*
>
> (E)

The body I am addressing and God's Word is addressing is a body, a governing body that is going to be brought forth out of all the unsaved nations (Gentiles, a people not in covenant with the living God), and Messianic Jews into "...One nation under God, indivisible..." *the Church, the household of faith* (Ephesians 2:22, Galatians 6:10).

A Church United Spiritually, Domestically, And Economically

We, the church, as a family, a spiritual race of people, are coming together in this natural world through the anointing. We are a *Super-Natural Church*, composed of *Super-Natural People*, doing *Super-Natural things* through the *Super-Natural power of God (the Anointing). The purpose of the Anointing* is to usher in the Savior who will be returning for His Church (Church: def., *Governing body by spiritual authority*) that will reign with him in the new millennium, *the "true" Age of The Church.* We will prepare by coming together (1) Spiritually, (2) Domestically, (3) Economically.

SPIRITUALLY:

We must take the thoughts of God and make them our own. We must allow his kingdom principles to be our way of life through the Anointing (Isaiah 55:8-13, Matthew 6:26, 33, Romans 8:1-2). Satan knew that if he could steal man's identity with God, we would be without hope (favorable expectation) and without God in the world

MANDATE OF THE ANOINTING

(Ephesians 2:11-12, 13). We would be void of true purpose and an easy prey to destroy (2 Tim.2:26). God sent His Son to pave the way for us, "Ben-Adam," *God's type of a MAN* to once again link up with Him and our true identity and purpose. Christ Jesus, through His death and resurrection, made the Anointing legally accessible to every man (Romans 10:13, 2 Corinthians 10:21, Matthew 28:19-20).

In Christ, we take back what Satan has stolen, our purpose, identity, and wealth (John 10:10).

DOMESTICALLY:

As men and women of God, we must take our role as husbands and wives, fathers and mothers, and sisters and brothers. We need to know what it is to be a family, first at home and then as a church. The church cannot thrive in power until we first know how to thrive as a natural family in our homes as Christian families in a dark world. We are the light of the world, the light that they (the lost in the world) will run to as they see the blessings of God manifesting in our lives.

When the sinner sees the love, peace, and safety of God's presence in our lives and homes, when the sinner sees the prosperity of God in our lives and in our businesses, and the favor of God we have on our jobs, and, when the sinner sees how blessed we are in everything we put our hands to, *we will not have to pursue the sinner* to reach him, *because he will pursue us.*

In Christ, men will no longer become victimized and spiritually beheaded by Satan, whose purpose is to destroy their families, their wives, and children through his deadly plots of destruction.

Those that are women will no longer be abused and prostituted in life. They will not be robbed of their opportunity to fulfill and complete their lives. In Christ, they will obtain their true purpose and rise above the curse of satanic insecurity and forced submission. As women born and inspired by God, they will fulfill their mandate in marriage to godly men that will love, protect, and provide the godly environment for their wives and children as well as themselves, no longer suffering through spiritual ignorance; they will know their role as wife and mother. *Spiritual knowledge reveals true identity and purpose.*

These God-inspired, God-led women will no longer be entangled with the yoke of bondage (Galatians 5:1), but rather they will perform as Godly wives and walk-in motherly love toward their children. They will provide an environment of safety, peace, and truth. These women will be mothers that will teach and raise their children to love and reverence God. These women will be mothers that will protect their children from the heartless, wicked designs of the evil one and bring them up to know the true and living God through the Word.

In Christ, we become the role models our children need to pattern their lives and succeed. In Christ, as godly parents living godly principles before our children, we will have fewer broken homes and families as a result of a right relationship with God.

Those who have allowed Satan to destroy their relationships must trust God to help them to restore what Satan has destroyed (Joel 2:25-28). Like Legion in the Book of St. Mark, Jesus will deliver us from our *swine-life bondage* and free us to "go home" and *take our proper positions in our homes as Fathers and Mothers, as well as leaders in our community.* We men will become the head and covering of our families while at the same time becoming a light to the world. Women will walk in their office of a wife not as inferior vessels but as a "face to face" compliment to her husband, and feminine head of the household, as well as mother to her children.

Single men and women of God must be holy, live Godly clean lives *through the Anointing* and avoid fornication, and taking advantage of having to answer to God only and not to a spouse. Allow God, through His Anointing, to use you to the utter most to deliver those that are in the gutter most.

This is what *the purpose of the anointing* is in the church: *to restore* our lives and *to fulfill the purpose* of the

Lord Advocate General of the Church, Jesus *guiding us, the Church into unity,* as the *body of Christ,* the head of the Church. A church (a spirit life nation), under God, indivisible, with liberty, and justice (righteousness of God through Christ Jesus) for all the Church, which is His body (Ephesians 1:3-23). *Praise God! Hallelujah!*

ECONOMICALLY:

The Word declares:

> But thou shalt remember the Lord thy God: for *it is* he that giveth thee power to get wealth, that he may establish his covenant which he sware unto thy fathers, as *it is* this day.
>
> Deuteronomy 8:18

As the church begins to take its rightful place as the body of Christ, as we begin to implement the laws of God, God will impart his wisdom to obtain wealth, for wisdom produces wealth. Note Psalm 112:

> 1 Praise ye the Lord. Blessed is the man *that* feareth the Lord that delighteth greatly in his commandments. 2 His seed shall be mighty upon the earth: The generation of the upright shall be blessed. 3 Wealth and riches *shall be*

in his house: and his righteousness endureth
for ever.

Psalm 112:1-3

As a child of God, you will be blessed, that is *empowered to prosper as it pertains to the ways and means of God, both spiritually and naturally*, and obtain wealth because he will govern his life according to the law of the Lord. His household and family shall abide in wealth.

Here we see that God intends not only for us to be *holy* but *whole* as well. *This is true salvation*, soundness, wholeness, wealth, prosperity, nothing missing, and nothing broken. The Greek word[s] for this description is sōzō [*save[d]*], sōtēria [*Salvation*] (Acts 4:12).

The church, as an economic force in the earth, in the last days, will reach out like never before in known history. The Church will fulfill Scripture; they will look up, and they will all see him, the manifested Christ, because he will be preached throughout the whole world, the Anointed and His message of deliverance and peace (Habakkuk 2:14, Matthew 24:14-35).

The church will become that governing body prophesied by the Christ himself in Matthew 16:18: "upon this rock I will build my church [governing body]," a Church that is complete, sound, whole and prosperous in every way, spiritually, materially, and naturally.

Man's Uniqueness and Dependence upon the Anointing

Man is the most *unique being upon the earth*. He is superior and far above every living thing upon the face of the earth. The rest of creation, specifically animals, are wonderfully created in every way, regardless of the species. However, animals all function as a result of instinct. Man, however, *the Homo sapiens, must be taught, guided, and molded* into the *Character* that will insure they will be *a contribution and not instruments of destruction*. That is why *the Gospel of Jesus Christ is so vital to man;* without its *power of regeneration,* super-naturally recreating man, *from his fallen spiritual state,* he will inevitably become an *instrument potentially of intense destruction.*

Man submitted to God becomes *the body of Christ, the Church* in the earth *revealing the mysteries [hidden plans] of the living God* (Ephesians 3:10). This man, in Christ, begins to *fulfill his true purpose or destiny [the Mandate of the Anointing]*. Every man has a purpose, or he would never been allowed to come to planet earth. If you entered the womb and exited the birth canal, *God has a plan and purpose for you.* Note Jeremiah 1:5:

> 5 "Before I shaped you in the womb,
> *I knew all about you.*
> Before you saw the light of day,
> *I had holy plans for you:*

A prophet to the nations—
that's what I had in mind for you."

(MSG Translation) (E)

Continuing with the original thought, this is the *uniqueness of man*; he is the *only creature* created in *the image of God*. This is *man's dependence*; due to the fall of Adam, *he [man] must be born again and of the Spirit of Christ* (the *last* Adam). This *new birth* enables this *new man* to live a *new life* submitted to *the Word of God; Christ [The Anointed and His Anointing], re-incarnated in him, the believer,* that is "Christ in you the hope of glory" (Colossians 1:27). This new man is *procreating the Gospel of the Anointed and revealing his Anointing* not only to other men and women but to the angels and spirits throughout the spiritual realm (Ephesians 3:7-10).

In addition, this *new man* will subdue the lawless one, Satan himself. The body of Christ composed of these *new men and women of God,* the *Church* will make him (Satan) the footstool of the Christ Himself, and indeed, place Satan under Jesus' feet, through the body of Christ (Hebrews 1:10-13, 14, Ephesians 1:16-22).

Now, in order to *fulfill this mandate,* we must divorce ourselves of erroneous thinking and teachings that "money is the root of all evil." The Bible never said that nor taught that, but rather, it taught "...the love of money is the root of all evil..." (1 Timothy 6:10). In other words, it is not *we possessing money* that is evil, rather it is *money possessing us,* and money is *a hard taskmaster.*

The Word of God says in Psalm 35:27:

> Let them shout for joy, and be glad, let them say continually, let the Lord be magnified, which *hath pleasure in the prosperity of his servant.*
>
> (E)

So you see, *it's God's will that we prosper in order to promote His cause on the earth.* You cannot do that without money. *As long as we live in this world, it will take money to get things done. We must believe that God wants to prosper us the Church,* or He will not be able to transfer the wealth into our hands (Proverbs 13:22[b]). We cannot expect God to bless us with something that is evil, and if money is evil, why does He express His pleasure and purpose in us having it?

Now granted, God does not desire to prosper us just to heap upon ourselves, but rather *to finance and procreate the Gospel of Jesus Christ.* I believe as long as we put God first and His purpose for our lives, the residue alone of those financial blessings will be *more than enough* to supply our every need. I believe this because His name is *El Shaddai, the God of more than enough.*

The Bible says Godly men prosper; note Psalm 112:

1 Praise ye the Lord. Blessed is the man that fearth the Lord, that delighteth greatly in his *commandments (Word)*. 2 His seed shall be mighty upon the earth: the generation of the upright shall *be blessed (empowered to prosper)*. 3 *Wealth and riches shall be in his house:* and his righteousness endureth for ever.

Psalm 112:1-3 (E)

Based on the above passage, you can say, in reality, it goes along with the lifestyle. As a mentor of mine once stated (paraphrasing), "you can't get the water without the wet." You see, water is wet and you can't have water without the wet. It comes along with the water.

The world refers to them that are rich in this world, "the lifestyle of the rich and famous," but in our dispensation, as believers in the Word of God, the phrase will change to "The Lifestyle of the Blessed and Wealthy." Praise God!!!

The time is now! The Word of God declares, "for the kingdom of God is at hand" (Available now, to him that believes), this is the day when the world will look up and say, "I want to be like them, "the blessed and wealthy, I want to know their God and be blessed."

A mentor of mine stated (paraphrase), "...Time will no longer tell our faith when, but rather our faith will tell time when..." Isaiah says it so:

1 Arise [change your posture and your position], shine; for thy light is come, and the glory of the Lord is risen upon thee. 2 For, behold, the darkness shall cover the earth, and gross darkness the people: but the Lord shall arise upon thee, and his glory shall be seen upon thee. 3 And the Gentiles shall come to thy light, and kings to the brightness of thy rising. 4 Lift up thine eye round about, and see: all they gather themselves together, they come to thee: thy sons shall come from far, and thy daughters shall be nursed at thy side. 5 Then thou shalt see, and flow together, and thine heart shall fear, and be enlarged; because the abundance of the sea shall be converted unto thee, the forces [wealth] of the Gentiles shall come unto thee [my covenant people].

Isaiah 60:1-5 (E)

A Church Equipped For Ministry

For many years we have gotten ministry backwards. Many of us who were called to ministry tried to build a ministry without money and just Holiness (I was one of them). We didn't realize it was God's will that we submit our lives to Him, pursue the wisdom to get wealth, that we may establish our ministry to establish His covenant in the earth (Deuteronomy 8:18). Note Joel chapter 2, verses 21-32:

> 21 Fear not, O land; be glad and rejoice: for the Lord will do great things. 22 Be not afraid, ye beasts of the field: for the pastures of the wilderness do spring, for the tree beareth her fruit...23 Be glad then ye children of Zion, and rejoice in the Lord your God: for he hath given you the former rain moderately, and he will cause to come down for you the rain, the former rain, and the latter rain in the *first month*.

In other words, the last shall be better than the first,

> 24 And the floors shall be full of wheat, and the vats shall be full of wheat, and the vats shall overflow with wine and oil. 25 And I will restore to you the years that the locust hath eaten, the cankerworm, and the caterpiller, and the palmerworm, my great army which I sent among you. 26 And ye shall eat in plenty, and be satisfied, and praise the name of the Lord your God that hath dealt wondrously with you: and my people shall never be ashamed.

> 27 And ye shall know that I *am*...the Lord your
> God...and my people shall never be ashamed.

These passages indicate God shall prosper you and bless you above all the nations. You shall never be an offense, disappointed or ashamed. In short, "you shall be the head and not the tail" (Deuteronomy 28:8-13).

In other words, then we will begin to move forth in ministry. And if I may be permitted to add, you are living in those days at this very present moment. This Scripture is more at the point of fulfilling now than at any other time in the history of humanity. Praise God! It is imperative that we allow the Holy Spirit to renew our thinking now!

Continuing from Joel 2:28-32:

> 28 And it shall come to pass afterward, that
> I will pour out my spirit upon all flesh; and
> your sons and your daughters shall proph-
> esy, your old men shall dream dreams, your
> young men shall see visions: 29 And also
> upon the servants and upon the handmaids
> in those days will I pour out my spirit 30 And
> I will shew wonders in the heavens and in the
> earth, blood, and fire, and pillars of smoke.
> 31 The sun shall be turned into darkness, and
> the moon into blood, before the great and ter-

rible day of the LORD come. 32 And it shall come to pass *that* whosoever shall call on the name of the Lord shall be delivered (saved; made whole, complete, sound, wealthy, and at peace; *that is nothing missing and nothing broken*): for in mount Zion and in Jerusalem shall be deliverance (Salvation), as the Lord hath said, and in the remnant whom the Lord shall call.

(E)

We see in verses 28 through 32 that "afterwards," or *after* He has equipped us financially, through His wisdom and power *reigning* in our lives, He begins to utilize us to proclaim the *kingdom of God*, and that the message is to be proclaimed through all generations, until that great and notable day of His return (vs. 31). The task is foreseeable because He has blessed or empowered us to obtain wealth. He provides us with "more than enough" to *promote, finance, expand, and build* successful ministries to bring in the harvest.

However, the end result is for all His covenant people and those that hear them to experience God's salvation; "nothing missing and nothing broken, that means peace and wealth." He has saved *the best for last!* (vs. 32).

By now, we should see the significance of receiving God's Word concerning wealth. There is a great mandate that requires us to believe, accept, and pursue it. *Do not accept "no" for an answer.* As His covenant people, it is our right, it is ours, and *we shall not be denied.* The Lord of the Host (*Sabaoth*) desires you to reap your harvest and is willing to see that it comes to pass with his host of spiritual angels. *We are the remnant* that Joel prophesied of, *who will believe God at His Word* and go forth in His name and take a land and take a people.

I feel it so significant to add, isn't it miraculously awesome that in Luke 4:18, that the first thing on Jesus' agenda is our welfare? For he stood and read, in what is recorded as Isaiah chapter 61:1: "The Spirit of the LORD is upon me, because...*he has anointed me to preach the gospel to the poor...*" Is it not, because he was first concerned about *changing their posture and their position both, materially and then spiritually* (Isaiah 60:1-5)?

Therefore the word "afterward," reflected in Joel 2:28, emphasizes *a shift in time and in position,* and begins to address the more spiritual issues at hand (Note both passages, Isaiah 61:1-2, and Luke 4:18-19); this has always been on the forefront of God's mind (Old and New Covenant):

> 11 For I know the thoughts that I think toward you, saith the LORD, thoughts of peace, and not of evil, to give you an expected end.
>
> Jeremiah 29:11

Even as Jesus declared, in Matthew chapter 11, verse 12:

>...The kingdom of heaven suffereth violence, and the violent take it by force...

He went on to declare in verse 25:

>...I thank thee, O Father, Lord of heaven and earth, because thou hast hid these things from the wise and prudent, and hast revealed them unto babes...

In other words, Jesus is referring to the believers willing to be taught the wisdom of God to fulfill His mandate "both to will and to do of his good pleasure" (Philippians 2:13).

Matthew 11:29 continues:

>Take my yoke upon you, and learn of me, for I am meek and lowly in heart: and ye shall find rest unto your souls.

He invites the babes to come and *learn my way of doing things.* You will find *peace of mind.* So is *the mandate of*

the Anointing, to *teach the teachable and anoint them to do.*
The Time Is Now!

Jesus said, in Matthew 7:24-25:

> 24 Therefore whosoever *heareth these sayings*
> *(The Word)* of mine, and <u>doeth</u> them, I will
> liken him unto a *wise man*, which *built his*
> *house upon a rock*: 25 And the rain descended,
> and the floods came, and the winds blew, and
> beat upon that house, *and it fell not*: for it was
> *founded upon a rock*.
>
> (E)

So you see, the man that hears and believes the
Word, that is, hear and do the Word, is the one who
gains the wisdom to prosper and successfully deal wise-
ly in the affairs of life. This is the Church that Christ
(the Anointed and His Anointing) is returning for, and
the Anointing has a mandate, a destiny, if you will, concerning the Church, to bring this Word to full fruition
in the Church, this is the will of the Father concerning
the Church (Ephesians 1:4-5, 9, 5:25-27).

CHAPTER 10

The Resurrected Church

A Close Encounter of the God Kind

In Apostle Paul's letter to the Church in Philippi (Philippians 3:1-14), it reflects what I personally believe is *the mandate of God's Anointing in and upon us*. That mandate is like Christ: we reach that state where we no longer live for ourselves, but for *the God-Head* (God, the Anointed, and His Anointing), realizing God's purpose and calling for our lives to the extent where nothing else matters.

Apostle Paul had reached the apex of his ministry. He yearned to experience a fellowship with the Anointing that would allow him to experience the zenith of what Christ Jesus Himself experienced in his resurrected body. This desire was so strong within Paul. I believe it was the most compelling drive within him. A drive so intense until it produced an anointing and favor, totally without his knowledge in the natural, to be chosen to write three-quarters of the New Covenant.

As shocking as it may sound, although he was once a persecutor of the Church (Acts 7:54-8:3, 9:1-2), why was this man chosen to write three-quarters of the New Covenant? How could this be? Well, first of all, he was not the same man he was prior to his *Damascus road (his spiritual reborn state)* experience (Acts 9:3-16, 13:1-13). That person, *the persecutor, died* on the Damascus road, and the *new Saul, now Paul,* underwent *A Close Encounter of the God Kind.* Now, this new, born again Paul had a quest for God in knowledge of truth (Philippians 4:10). When you meet truth, or rather the truth is revealed to you, you will never fall for religion ever again; it's literally impossible (Hebrews 6:4-6, Galatians 4:4-9).

Therefore, the Paul we see in the letter to the Philippians is a *far cry* from the man prior to the Damascus road encounter. Praise God! Paul is now a man on a quest that transcends the natural. His desire has become supernatural. He is a man that dwells in another realm, living under a new law (Romans 8:1-2). He was now a man without a past: "we (those who have received the promises through the righteousness of God by faith) have wronged no man" (2 Corinthians 7:2). In fact, if you have ever notice in any of Apostle Paul's letters to the church, after the first, two, or three verses, he is *a man speaking from his spirit and not his intellect.*

There isn't much we can do for God in the flesh except crucify it and *submit it broken before God* (1 Corinthians 9:24-27, Romans 12:1-2, James 4:7-10). I also believe this is why Paul preached *the Righteousness of God* with such a conviction it encompassed two-thirds of his letters to the Church. Without this revelation, we couldn't walk in the *reality of righteousness*; it would be impossible to receive the Promises of God without this revelation. It is no way we could account ourselves worthy short of *righteousness by faith*.

Note Philippians 3:9-11:

> 9 And be found in him, not having mine own righteousness, which is of the law, but that which is through *the faith of Christ, the righteousness* which is of *God by faith*: 10 That I may know him, and the power of his resurrection, and the fellowship of his sufferings, being made conformable unto his death; 11 If by any means I might attain unto the resurrection of the dead.
>
> (E)

The Apostle Paul knew in his heart that in order to reach this ideal, it required a relationship with the Christ (The Anointing), *the very person of the Spirit who abided in and upon the Lord*, for Paul knew that it was *this*

155

embodiment that enabled Christ (The Anointed) *to fulfill the call of God on His life.* Somehow Paul knew this was to be *God's ultimate goal for every man* (Ephesians 1:9-23).

Paul knew this would be controversial; that is why he ascribed in a previous passage of the same letter (Philippians):

> 5 Let this mind be in you, which was also in Christ Jesus: 6 Who, being in the form of God, thought is not robbery to be equal with God...
>
> Philippians 2:5-6

Also, in subsequent passages of Philippians:

> 15 Let us therefore, as many as be perfect [mature], be thus minded [should be of the same mind]; and if in any thing ye be otherwise minded [be of a different mind], God shall reveal even this [or make this conviction clear] unto you. 16 Nevertheless, whereto we have already attained [of the same mind], let us walk by the same rule, let us mind the same thing [move forward on what we do agree].
>
> Philippians 3:15-16 (E)

It was clear that Apostle Paul was no longer concerned about what people thought. He defined the plane from which he declared his conviction, *which was the Scriptures and the Gospel of Christ, the New Covenant revealed in his spirit by the Holy Spirit* (The Anointing). His desire was that those in the new church that agreed with him, in unity they continue to move forward to pursue this spiritual truth in their lives. Also, to those of the church that had a contradictory conviction, he declared that with sincere hearts, that through growth of their relationship in Christ, this same conviction would eventually be revealed likewise to them.

Paul desired to draw near to God, even as Moses had desired in the wilderness (Ex.33:18-34:9). He often referred in his letters of this conviction within him, of his acclamation of the revelation of the Christ (1 Timothy 6:16, 13-15, Romans 1:1-4, 2 Corinthians 4:6-7, 10-12, 14, 16-17, 18).

The Resurrected Life

What promoted or prompted this conviction in Paul, was it his intellect? No, a thousand times no. It was *the fellowship of the Spirit* (note 1 Corinthians 1:4-9, 10[a], Philippians 2:1-2). The determined purpose of Apostle Paul to lay aside everything that would come between him and the Christ gave birth to this *supernatural quest* to know his Savior. He was consumed with the desire to experience the *resurrected life*, even while in his mortal body, and its reward (Philippians 3:11, 10-14).

We will one day in the millennium come to fully understand this when those that will be the survivors of the tribulation period look upon us, the church, that escape the tribulation through faith in the Anointed and His Anointing.

When they witness us as we come and go in our resurrected bodies, they will not really recognize us until we do something that only those in resurrected bodies can do. We in resurrected bodies will walk through walls, not bothering to open doors or ascending stairs. We will be able to transport ourselves from one point to another in the twinkling of an eye. In fact, we will be able to do everything Jesus did when He was resurrected from the dead in His resurrected body. Those of them in mortal bodies will say, "That's one of them! Did you see that?...he just walked through the wall" or "She vanished right before my eyes." Praise God! Talk about "Beam me up Scotty," *I know a better way: live in the Anointing of the Anointed.*

Changed Into another Man

Well, I believe Paul had this *compassion* to experience this existence, even while in his mortal body (Philippians 3:11). This often makes me think of the lyrics in a well-known Christian praise, "don't wait for the victory, shout now!"

What then is the resolve of all of this, you may ask? All that Jesus did while in the earth, He has passed the baton to you (the Church) to continue until His return. He has not left us ill-equipped because He has left *His Word, His Name, and His Anointing*. As Caleb declared, "for we are well able to overcome it [possess the land]" (Numbers 13:30). He gave us everything to experience the Anointed life.

The Greater One in You

The Greater one lives in us, the Anointing of the Anointed. He is *greater than Satan, and his demon hosts that are rulers of this world's darkness* (1 John 4:4, 1-7, Ephesians 6:10-13, 14-18, 19), and He, the Anointing, lives and abides in and upon you. We can rise above every reproach, obstacle, challenge, or satanic strategy, through the Anointing and wisdom of the living God (Isaiah 54:14-17, 10:27). *The Anointing is the solution to every burden and every yoke.*

He is here now, to reveal, to assist, *to change you into another man*. When the Anointing rested upon Saul, he was *changed into another man* (1 Samuel 10:1-6, 7). As Jabez said, "that thy hand might be with me" (1 Chronicles 4:10). When the Anointing is with you, God's presence:

God's glory is present to do far over and above anything you could ever ask or even think, in you, for you and through you (Ephesians 3:20-21).

He is available to accomplish the Will of God through you "Christ in you, the hope of Glory" (Colossians 1:27[b]). You will become another man, a man that will walk in power, the resurrected power of God to obtain all that will empower you to accomplish the purpose of your earthly destiny. The Anointing will enable you to know yourself and your destiny in God's plan (Romans 8:29). *His plan for your life is the image of his Son, the Anointed, all over again.*

God Has a Plan

What is your decision? Will you choose to submit to the Anointing, who knows God's plan for your life (see Deuteronomy 30:19-20)?

Observe Jerimiah 29:11-14:

> 11 For I know the thoughts that I think toward you, saith the Lord, thoughts of peace, and not of evil, to give you an expected end...14... and I will turn away your captivity, and I will gather you from all the nations...

God has a plan for you; if you desire to know it, *pursue Jesus and His Anointing.* God's plan for you was laid out for you before the foundation of the world. And they are plans of welfare, peace, and purpose for being.

If you feel you have no purpose for being, it is because you have not acquainted yourself with *the one that knows all things* and *knows you better than you know yourself.* He is able to give purpose to your being, and He will assist you in accomplishing it. As Paul declared, you will do the same: "I can do all things through Christ [The Anointing and His Anointed] which strengthens [equips, qualifies and commissions] me" (Philippians 4:13), *The Mandate of The Anointing.*

A Covenant of Better Promises

Don't ever forget that *the Anointing is a Person,* sent to be with you *to empower you for every challenge in life,* in order to *restore* God's purpose for you in the earth and the worlds to come. He is here to teach you how *to live like, think like, and be like God.* He is your surety, *a down payment on better things to come* (Ephesians 1:11-14), he is the *evidence of a better covenant of better promises* (Hebrews 8:6), *with better sacrifices* (Hebrews 9:23-24), *and a more enduring substance* (Hebrews 10:34), *the faith of Jesus, and His Anointing.* Those promises are available to you now, through Him that has called you from darkness unto light!

My prayer for the *entire body of Christ* is that they may come to know the *Mandate of the Anointing*. Jesus came to know his purpose for being in the earth, to *fulfill God's plan* to redeem man from the fall. And He (Christ) came that you may come to know *your purpose* the same way. God desires for you and me *to know our purpose and calling*:

> 18 The Spirit of the Lord is upon me, because he hath anointed me to preach the gospel to the poor; he hath sent me to heal the broken-hearted, to preach deliverance to the captives, and recovering of sight to the blind, to set at liberty them that are bruised, 19 To preach the acceptable year of the Lord.
>
> Luke 4:18-19

Now He says to you, *You are the light [those illuminated by the Word of Life]*, and like Him, as long as we are in the world, we should *let our light [of the Anointing on us]* so shine before men, that they may see our good works, *glorifying our Father in heaven*:

> ...be blameless and harmless, *the sons of God*, without rebuke, in the midst of a crooked and

perverse nation, among *whom ye shine as lights in the world...*

Philippians 2:15[b] (E)

You have a personal responsibility as men and women of God to seek the fellowship of the Spirit, the Anointing, and His Anointed, that you, like our Savior Christ Jesus, may fulfill your destiny, *"The Mandate of The Anointing."*

CPSIA information can be obtained
at www.ICGtesting.com
Printed in the USA
BVHW040101210521
607644BV00020B/768